Joe Gould's Secret

JOE GOULD

JOE GOULD'S SECRET

SECRET

JOSEPH MITCHELL

Introduction by William Maxwell

THE MODERN LIBRARY

NEW YORK

2000 Modern Library Edition

Introduction © 1996 by William Maxwell
Biographical note copyright © 1992 by Random House, Inc.
"Professor Sea Gull" copyright © 1942 by Joseph Mitchell
"Joe Gould's Secret" copyright © 1964 by Joseph Mitchell

"Professor Sea Gull" originally appeared in the December 12, 1942,
issue of *The New Yorker.*
"Joe Gould's Secret" originally appeared in the September 19 and 26, 1964,
issues of *The New Yorker.*

Illustrations by Saul Steinberg copyright © 1964 by The New Yorker
Magazine. Reprinted by permission of Saul Steinberg.

MODERN LIBRARY and colophon are registered
trademarks of Random House, Inc.

Library of Congress Cataloging-in-Publication Data
Mitchell, Joseph, 1908–1996
Joe Gould's secret/Joseph Mitchell.
p.   cm.
ISBN 0-679-60339-5
1. Gould, Joe, 1889–1957. 2. Eccentrics and eccentricities—New
York (N.Y.)—Biography. 3. New York (N.Y.)—Biography. I. Title.
CT9991.G6M5   1996
974.7'104'092—dc20   95-35285

Modern Library website address: www.modernlibrary.com

Printed in the United States of America on acid-free paper

2 4 6 8 9 7 5 3 1

JOSEPH MITCHELL

Joseph Mitchell came to New York City from a small farming town named Fairmont in the swamp country of southeastern North Carolina in 1929, when he was twenty-one years old, looking for a job as a newspaper reporter. He arrived at Pennsylvania Station on Friday, October 25, the day after the stock-market crash that is generally considered to have been the beginning of the Great Depression. He eventually managed to find a job as a kind of bottom-depths apprentice crime reporter at Police Headquarters for *The World*. He worked as a reporter and feature writer—for *The World, The Herald Tribune,* and *The World-Telegram*—for eight years, and then went to *The New Yorker,* where he remained until his death at the age of eighty-seven.

Aside from writing, Mr. Mitchell's particular interests were the waterfront of New York City, commercial fishing, Gypsies, Southern agriculture, Irish literature, and the architecture of New York City. He served several terms on the board of directors of the Gypsy Lore Society, an international organization of students of Gypsy life and

the Gypsy language, founded in England in 1888. *Bajour,*
a musical comedy written by someone else but based on
stories about Gypsies by Mitchell, ran for 232 perfor-
mances on Broadway in 1964–65. An architecture buff, he
frequently spent a day wandering around the city with a
pair of binoculars studying the façades of old buildings.
He was one of the founders of the South Street Seaport
Museum, he was one of the original friends of the Friends
of Cast-Iron Architecture, and for five years he was one of
the Commissioners of the New York City Landmarks
Preservation Commission. His favorite institutions in the
city were the Metropolitan Museum, Fulton Fish Market,
the Grand Central Oyster Bar, McSorley's alehouse,
Grace Church, the Belmont racetrack, the Staten Island
ferry, the Gotham Book Mart (he attended meetings of
the James Joyce Society on the second floor of the
Gotham for thirty years), and the William T. Davis
Wildlife Refuge in the Staten Island marshes. Increas-
ingly over the years he went back to North Carolina,
spending months at a time down there helping reforest
some cut-over timberland and worn-out farmland along
the edge of Ashpole Swamp, going into the swamp now
and then to look for wildflowers and for woodpeckers and
hawks, his favorite birds. Once, deep in the swamp, looking through binoculars, he watched for an hour or so as a
pileated woodpecker tore the bark off the upper trunk

and limbs of a tall old dead blackgum tree, and he said he considered this the most spectacular event he had ever witnessed.

Mr. Mitchell was married to Therese Mitchell the photographer; they had two daughters, Nora Sanborn of Eatontown, New Jersey, and Elizabeth Curtis, of Atlanta, Georgia, and three granddaughters, two grandsons, and one great-granddaughter.

Therese Mitchell died in 1980. Joseph Mitchell died May 24, 1996.

INTRODUCTION TO THE
COMMEMORATIVE EDITION
OF *JOE GOULD'S SECRET*

by William Maxwell

The two parts of *Joe Gould's Secret* were originally published, with a twenty-two-year interval between them, as
Profiles in *The New Yorker.* They were then published as
a book, with an author's note that is brief but revealing: It
begins "This book consists of two views of the same man,
a lost soul named Joe Gould." Consider the word
"views"—the farthest possible remove from the dogmatic,
though as a portrait the two Profiles are surely definitive.
Gould was a Greenwich Village character who, when he
was not pursuing the bee in his bonnet, went from bar to
bar cadging money and drinks off friends and strangers.
He must have been known to hundreds of people, few of
whom would have been charitable enough to describe
him as a lost soul, though he unquestionably was one.

Over a period of many years Joseph Mitchell listened to
him, in saloons and cafeterias, sometimes for eight or ten
hours at a stretch and once until four o'clock in the morning. His description of Gould—"an odd and penniless and
unemployable little man who came to the city in 1916 and
ducked and dodged and held on as hard as he could for

over thirty-five years" reminds me of the sound carpenters make when they are building a house. *Bung, bung, bung, kapung, kapung, kapung.* No hesitations. No bent nails. Every word driven, so to speak, all the way into the wood.

In the second section of the book, the process of interviewing, as a rule impersonal and unemotional, was neither of these things. It has so much about Mitchell—his habits and scruples, what he hoped to accomplish and what he was afraid might happen—that it seems at times to be as much about him as it is about Gould, and could almost be taken for a double Profile. To the best of my knowledge this had never been done before and constitutes a breakthrough: the Reporter as Human Being.

Usually when Profile reporters have published a piece they sever whatever personal ties they have formed with the subject and what may have seemed like the beginning of a friendship, but year after year Mitchell went on handing out small sums of money and listening to Gould, out of *courtesy.* This can perhaps be accounted for by his Southern upbringing. His father was a cotton buyer and owned a tobacco and cotton farm. Mitchell grew up in comfortable circumstances in North Carolina. His ancestors were farming in the region before the American Revolution. Or it could have been merely a reflection of his own nature. If pressed, and especially in the face of prying questions about work in progress, he could be fierce and formidable, but he was essentially a sweet-natured man. I loved talking to him. He seldom managed to finish his sentences because of all the relevant qualifying thoughts that rushed into his mind. It didn't matter. It was still communication, but of a higher, all-inclusive kind. I loved looking at him because of the light in his eye and his smile, which became broad and joyful when he remembered some extreme oddity of human behavior. He didn't appear to be anywhere near his age and moved with a lightness uncommon in old men. Though he no longer believed in the theological tenets of the Baptist Church, he continued to look at life from a religious viewpoint. Mortality was something he never lost sight of, and nothing gave him more pleasure than to wander about in an old graveyard reading the inscriptions on the tombstones.

I can't prove it but I suspect that he made a religion out of literature, with the great Irish novelist James Joyce as the presiding deity. In any case, writing—the art and practice of writing—didn't with him take second place to anything. I don't think he meant to outwrite everybody else in sight or much liked the worshiping admiration of younger *New Yorker* writers. He had a marvelous ear for speech and knew how to use it to project character, dramatize a moment, or frame a revelation. What more do you need to know in order to understand Joe Gould than his simple confession: "In my home town I never felt at home. I stuck out. Even in my own home, I never felt at home. In New York City, especially in Greenwich Village, down among the cranks and the misfits and the one-lungers and the has-beens and the might've-beens and the would-bes and the never-wills and the God-knows-whats, I have always felt at home."

As for Mitchell himself, it is somewhat odd that a person who could say "I have always deeply disliked seeing anyone shown up or found out or caught in a lie or caught red-handed doing anything" should have chosen to be a newspaper reporter. He solved the problem by giving way to his delight in and respect for people on the fringes of society. Gypsies, anarchists, quirky bartenders, Indians, deaf-mutes, street preachers, bearded ladies, child prodigies and prodigies of all kind he handled with the gentleness and protectiveness that you would handle a child.

In his story "The Cave Dwellers" Mitchell tells how, in the year 1933, the rock bottom of the Great Depression, he was working as a reporter on "a newspaper whose editors believed that nothing brightened up a front page so much as a story about human suffering." They sent him to breadlines, to relief bureaus, to evictions, and to stand beside the Salvation Army bell-ringers. Somebody wrote in to the paper about an unemployed carpenter and his wife who in the dead of winter were living in a cave in Central

Park. By the time Mitchell caught up with them a good Samaritan had lodged them in a furnished room. Mitchell's piece about them, about their efforts to keep from starving or freezing to death, ran just before Christmas and brought a flood of letters, some of them containing money or a check, and two telegrams offering a job. When Mitchell went to see them two days later the landlady appeared to be angry and told him that people who had seen the article had been bringing food and money all day. When he got upstairs he found their room in disorder and the cave people quite drunk.

"It's that sneak from the newspaper," the woman said.

"What do you mean printing lies about us in the paper?" the man said. "You said we had only seven cents left, you liar."

"I told you we had *seventy* cents," the woman said.

The man got a good grip on a bottle of gin and Mitchell said, edging toward the door, "Wait a minute. I brought you some money."

"I don't want your money," the man said. "I got money."

"Well," Mitchell said, holding out the telegrams, "I think I got a job for you."

"I don't want your help," the man said. "You put a lie about us in the paper."

Mitchell closed the door and hurried toward the stairs.

When he got as far as the landing of the second floor, the gin bottle struck the wall above his head and he was sprayed with gin and pieces of wet glass. When he got downstairs the landlady said, "What happened? What was that crash?"

"Mr. Holman threw a bottle of gin at me," Mitchell said. He was laughing.

He was one part angel.

To my sisters

ELIZABETH MITCHELL WOODWARD

LINDA MITCHELL LAMM

and

LAURA MITCHELL BRASWELL

with love

AUTHOR'S NOTE

This book consists of two views of the same man, a lost soul named Joe Gould. Both were written as Profiles for *The New Yorker*. I wrote the first, "Professor Sea Gull," in 1942, and it came out in the issue of December 12, 1942. Twenty-two years later, in 1964, I wrote the second, "Joe Gould's Secret," and it came out in the issues of September 19 and 26, 1964.

CONTENTS

PROFESSOR SEA GULL

Joe Gould is a blithe and emaciated little man who has been a notable in the cafeterias, diners, barrooms, and dumps of Greenwich Village for a quarter of a century. He sometimes brags rather wryly that he is the last of the bohemians. "All the others fell by the wayside," he says. "Some are in the grave, some are in the loony bin, and some are in the advertising business." Gould's life is by no means carefree; he is constantly tormented by what he calls "the three H's"—homelessness, hunger, and hangovers. He sleeps on benches in subway stations, on the floor in the studios of friends, and in quarter-a-night flophouses on the Bowery. Once in a while he trudges up to Harlem and goes to one of the establishments known as "Extension Heavens" that are operated by followers of Father Divine, the Negro evangelist, and gets a night's lodging for fifteen cents. He is five feet four and he hardly ever weighs more than a hundred pounds. Not long ago he told a friend that he hadn't eaten a square meal since June, 1936, when he bummed up to Cambridge and attended a banquet during a reunion of the Harvard class of 1911, of which he is a member. "I'm the foremost authority in the United States," he says, "on the subject of doing without." He tells people that he lives on "air, self-esteem, cigarette butts, cowboy coffee, fried-egg sandwiches, and ketchup." Cowboy coffee, he says, is strong coffee drunk black without sugar. "I've long since lost my taste for good coffee," he says. "I much prefer the kind that sooner or later, if you keep on drinking it, your hands will begin to shake and the whites of your eyes will turn yellow." While having a sandwich, Gould customarily empties a bottle or two of ketchup on his plate and eats it with a spoon. The countermen in the Jefferson Diner, on Village Square, which is one of his hangouts, gather up the ketchup bottles and hide them the moment he puts his head in the door. "I don't particularly like the confounded stuff," he says, "but I make it a practice to eat all I can get. It's the only grub I know of that's free of charge."

Gould is a Yankee. His branch of the Goulds has been in New England since 1635, and he is related to many of the other early New England families, such as the Lawrences, the Clarkes, and the Storers. "There's nothing accidental about me," he once said. "I'll tell you what it took to make me what I am today. It took old Yankee blood, an overwhelming aversion to possessions, four years of Harvard, and twenty-five years of beating the living hell out of my insides with bad hooch and bad food." He says that he is out of joint with the rest of the human race because he doesn't want to own anything. "If Mr. Chrysler tried to make me a present of the Chrysler Building," he says, "I'd damn near break my neck fleeing from him. I wouldn't own it; it'd own me. Back home in Massachusetts I'd be called an old Yankee crank. Here I'm called a bohemian. It's six of one, half a dozen of the other." Gould has a twangy voice and a Harvard accent. Bartenders and countermen in the Village refer to him as the Professor, the Sea Gull, Professor Sea Gull, the Mongoose, Professor Mongoose, or the Bellevue Boy. He dresses in the castoff clothes of his friends. His overcoat, suit, shirt, and even his shoes are all invariably a size or two too large, but he wears them with a kind of forlorn rakishness. "Just look at me," he says. "The only thing that fits is the necktie." On bitter winter days he puts a layer of

newspapers between his shirt and undershirt. "I'm snob-
bish," he says. "I only use the *Times*." He is fond of unusual headgear—a toboggan, a beret, or a yachting cap.
One summer evening he appeared at a party in a seersucker suit, a polo shirt, a scarlet cummerbund, sandals,
and a yachting cap, all hand-me-downs. He uses a long
black cigarette holder, and a good deal of the time he
smokes butts picked up off the sidewalks.

Bohemianism has aged Gould considerably beyond his
years. He has got in the habit lately of asking people he
has just met to guess his age. Their guesses range between
sixty-five and seventy-five; he is fifty-three. He is never
hurt by this; he looks upon it as proof of his superiority. "I
do more living in one year," he says, "than ordinary hu-
mans do in ten." Gould is toothless, and his lower jaw
swivels from side to side when he talks. He is bald on top,
but the hair at the back of his head is long and frizzly, and
he has a bushy, cinnamon-colored beard. He wears a pair
of spectacles that are loose and lopsided and that slip
down to the end of his nose a moment after he puts them
on. He doesn't always wear them on the street and without them he has the wild, unfocussed stare of an old
scholar who has strained his eyes on small print. Even in
the Village many people turn and look at him. He is
stooped and he moves rapidly, grumbling to himself, with

his head thrust forward and held to one side. Under his left arm he usually carries a bulging, greasy, brown pasteboard portfolio, and he swings his right arm aggressively. As he hurries along, he seems to be warding off an imaginary enemy. Don Freeman, the artist, a friend of his, once made a sketch of him walking. Freeman called the sketch "Joe Gould versus the Elements." Gould is as restless and footloose as an alley cat, and he takes long hikes about the city, now and then disappearing from the Village for weeks at a time and mystifying his friends; they have never been able to figure out where he goes. When he returns, always looking pleased with himself, he makes a few cryptic remarks, giggles, and then shuts up. "I went on a bird walk along the waterfront with an old countess," he said after his most recent absence. "The countess and I spent three weeks studying sea gulls."

Gould is almost never seen without his portfolio. He keeps it on his lap while he eats and in flophouses he sleeps with it under his head. It usually contains a mass of manuscripts and notes and letters and clippings and copies of obscure little magazines, a bottle of ink, a dictionary, a paper bag of cigarette butts, a paper bag of bread crumbs, and a paper bag of hard, round, dime-store candy of the type called sour balls. "I fight fatigue with sour balls," he says. The crumbs are for pigeons; like many

other eccentrics, Gould is a pigeon feeder. He is devoted
to a flock which makes its headquarters atop and around
the statue of Garibaldi in Washington Square. These pigeons know him. When he comes up and takes a seat on
the plinth of the statue, they flutter down and perch on his
head and shoulders, waiting for him to bring out his bag
of crumbs. He has given names to some of them. "Come
here, Boss Tweed," he says. "A lady in Stewart's Cafeteria
didn't finish her whole-wheat toast this morning and
when she went out, bingo, I snatched it off her plate especially for you. Hello, Big Bosom. Hello, Popgut. Hello,
Lady Astor. Hello, St. John the Baptist. Hello, Polly
Adler. Hello, Fiorello, you old goat, how're you today?"

Although Gould strives to give the impression that he
is a philosophical loafer, he has done an immense amount
of work during his career as a bohemian. Every day, even
when he has a bad hangover or even when he is weak and
listless from hunger, he spends at least a couple of hours
working on a formless, rather mysterious book that he
calls "An Oral History of Our Time." He began this book
twenty-six years ago, and it is nowhere near finished. His
preoccupation with it seems to be principally responsible
for the way he lives; a steady job of any kind, he says,
would interfere with his thinking. Depending on the
weather, he writes in parks, in doorways, in flophouse lob-

bies, in cafeterias, on benches on elevated-railroad platforms, in subway trains, and in public libraries. When he
is in the proper mood, he writes until he is exhausted, and
he gets into this mood at peculiar times. He says that one
night he sat for six or seven hours in a booth in a Third Avenue bar and grill, listening to a beery old Hungarian
woman, once a madam and once a dealer in narcotics and
now a soup cook in a city hospital, tell the story of her life.
Three days later, around four o'clock in the morning, on a
cot in the Hotel Defender, at 300 Bowery, he was awak-
ened by the foghorns of tugs on the East River and was
unable to go back to sleep because he felt that he was in
the exact mood to put the old soup cook's biography in his
history. He has an abnormal memory; if he is sufficiently
impressed by a conversation, he can keep it in his head,
even if it is lengthy and senseless, for many days, much of
it word for word. He had a bad cold, but he got up,
dressed under a red exit light, and, tiptoeing so as not to
disturb the men sleeping on cots all around him, went
downstairs to the lobby.

He wrote in the lobby from 4:15 A.M. until noon. Then
he left the Defender, drank some coffee in a Bowery
diner, and walked up to the Public Library. He plugged
away at a table in the genealogy room, which is one of his
rainy-day hangouts and which he says he prefers to the

main reading room because it is gloomier, until it closed at 6 P.M. Then he moved into the main reading room and stayed there, seldom taking his eyes off his work, until the Library locked up for the night at 10 P.M. He ate a couple of egg sandwiches and a quantity of ketchup in a Times Square cafeteria. Then, not having two bits for a flop-house and being too engrossed to go to the Village and seek shelter, he hurried into the West Side subway and rode the balance of the night, scribbling ceaselessly while the train he was aboard made three round trips between the New Lots Avenue station in Brooklyn and the Van Cortlandt Park station in the Bronx, which is one of the longest runs in the subway system. He kept his portfolio on his lap and used it as a desk. He has the endurance of the possessed. Whenever he got too sleepy to concen-trate, he shook his head vigorously and then brought out his bag of sour balls and popped one in his mouth. People stared at him, and once he was interrupted by a drunk who asked him what in the name of God he was writing. Gould knows how to get rid of inquisitive drunks. He pointed at his left ear and said, "What? What's that? Deaf as a post. Can't hear a word." The drunk lost all interest in him. "Day was breaking when I left the subway," Gould says. "I was coughing and sneezing, my eyes were sore, my knees were shaky, I was as hungry as a bitch wolf, and I had exactly eight cents to my name. I didn't care. My history was longer by eleven thousand brand-new words, and at that moment I bet there wasn't a chairman of the board in all New York as happy as I."

GOULD IS HAUNTED by the fear that he will die before he has the first draft of the Oral History finished. It is already eleven times as long as the Bible. He estimates that the manuscript contains 9,000,000 words, all in longhand. It may well be the lengthiest unpublished work in existence. Gould does his writing in nickel composition books, the kind that children use in school, and the Oral History and the notes he has made for it fill two hundred and seventy of them, all of which are tattered and grimy and stained with coffee, grease, and beer. Using a fountain pen, he covers both sides of each page, leaving no margins any-where, and his penmanship is poor; hundreds of thou-sands of words are legible only to him. He has never been able to interest a publisher in the Oral History. At one time or another he has lugged armfuls of it into fourteen publishing offices. "Half of them said it was obscene and outrageous and to get it out of there as quick as I could," he says, "and the others said they couldn't read my hand-writing." Experiences of this nature do not dismay Gould; he keeps telling himself that it is posterity he is writing for, anyway. In his breast pocket, sealed in a dingy envelope, he always carries a will bequeathing two-thirds of the manuscript to the Harvard Library and the other third to the Smithsonian Institution. "A couple of generations after I'm dead and gone," he likes to say, "the Ph.D.'s will start lousing through my work. Just imagine their surprise. 'Why, I be damned,' they'll say, 'this fellow was the most brilliant historian of the century.' They'll give me my due. I don't claim that all of the Oral History is first class, but some of it will live as long as the English language." Gould used to keep his composition books scattered all over the Village, in the apartments and studios of friends. He kept them stuck away in closets and under beds and behind the books in bookcases. In the winter of 1942, after hearing that the Metropolitan Museum had moved its most precious paintings to a bombproof storage place somewhere out of town for the duration of the war, he became panicky. He went around and got all his books together and made them into a bale, he wrapped the bale in two layers of oilcloth, and then he entrusted it to a woman he knows who owns a duck-and-chicken farm near Huntington, Long Island. The farmhouse has a stone cellar.

Gould puts into the Oral History only things he has seen or heard. At least half of it is made up of conversations taken down verbatim or summarized; hence the title. "What people say is history," Gould says. "What we used to think was history—kings and queens, treaties, inventions, big battles, beheadings, Caesar, Napoleon, Pontius Pilate, Columbus, William Jennings Bryan—is only formal history and largely false. I'll put down the informal history of the shirt-sleeved multitude—what they had to say about their jobs, love affairs, vittles, sprees, scrapes, and sorrows—or I'll perish in the attempt." The Oral History is a great hodgepodge and kitchen midden of hearsay, a repository of jabber, an omnium-gatherum of bushwa, gab, palaver, hogwash, flapdoodle, and malarkey, the fruit, according to Gould's estimate, of more than twenty thousand conversations. In it are the hopelessly incoherent biographies of hundreds of bums, accounts of the wanderings of seamen encountered in South Street barrooms, grisly descriptions of hospital and clinic experiences ("Did you ever have a painful operation or disease?" is one of the first questions that Gould, fountain pen and composition book in hand, asks a person he has just met), summaries of innumerable Union Square and Columbus Circle harangues, testimonies given by converts at Salvation Army street meetings, and the addled opinions of scores of park-bench oracles and gin-mill savants. For a time Gould haunted the all-night greasy spoons in the vicinity of Bellevue Hospital, eavesdropping on tired internes, nurses, orderlies, ambulance drivers, embalming-school students, and morgue workers, and faithfully recording their talk. He scurries up and down Fifth Avenue during parades, feverishly taking notes. Gould writes with great candor, and the percentage of obscenity in the Oral History is high. He has a chapter called "Examples of the So-called Dirty Story of Our Time," to which he makes almost daily additions. In another chapter are many rhymes and observations which he found scribbled on the walls of subway washrooms. He believes that these scribblings are as truly historical as the strategy of General Robert E. Lee. Hundreds of thousands of words are devoted to the drunken behavior and the sexual adventures of various professional Greenwich Villagers in the twenties. There are hundreds of reports of ginny Village parties, including gossip about the guests and faithful reports of their arguments on such subjects as reincarnation, birth control, free love, psychoanalysis, Christian Science, Swedenborgianism, vegetarianism, alcoholism, and different political and art isms. "I have fully covered what might be termed the intellectual underworld of my time," Gould says. There are detailed descriptions of night life in scores of Village drinking and eating places, some of which, such as the Little Quakeress, the Original Julius, the Troubadour Tavern, the Samovar, Hubert's Cafeteria, Sam Swartz's T.N.T., and Eli Greifer's Last Outpost of Bohemia Tea Shoppe, do not exist any longer.

Gould is a night wanderer, and he has put down descriptions of dreadful things he has seen on dark New York streets—descriptions, for example, of the herds of big gray rats that come out in the hours before dawn in some neighborhoods of the lower East Side and Harlem and unconcernedly walk the sidewalks. "I sometimes believe that these rats are not rats at all," he says, "but the damned and aching souls of tenement landlords." A great deal of the Oral History is in diary form. Gould is afflicted with total recall, and now and then he picks out a period of time in the recent past—it might be a day, a week, or a month—and painstakingly writes down everything of any consequence that he did during this period. Sometimes he writes a chapter in which he monotonously and hideously curses some person or institution. Here and there are rambling essays on such subjects as the flophouse flea, spaghetti, the zipper as a sign of the decay of civilization, false teeth, insanity, the jury system, remorse, cafeteria cooking, and the emasculating effect of the typewriter on literature. "William Shakespeare didn't sit around pecking on a dirty, damned, ninety-five-dollar doohickey," he wrote, "and Joe Gould doesn't, either."

The Oral History is almost as discursive as "Tristram Shandy." In one chapter, "The Good Men Are Dying Like Flies," Gould begins a biography of a diner proprietor and horse-race gambler named Side-Bet Benny Altschuler, who stuck a rusty icepick in his hand and died of lockjaw; and skips after a few paragraphs to a story a seaman told him about seeing a group of lepers drinking and dancing and singing on a beach in Port-of-Spain, Trinidad; and goes from that to an anecdote about a demonstration held in front of a moving-picture theatre in Boston in 1915 to protest against the showing of "The Birth of a Nation," at which he kicked a policeman; and goes from that to a description of a trip he once made through the Central Islip insane asylum, in the course of which a woman pointed at him and screamed, "There he is! Thief! Thief! There's the man that picked my geraniums and stole my mamma's mule and buggy"; and goes from that to an account an old stumble-bum gave of glimpsing and feeling the blue-black flames of hell one night while sitting in a doorway on Great Jones Street and of seeing two mermaids playing in the East River just north of Fulton Fish Market later the same night; and goes from that to an explanation made by a priest of Old St. Patrick's Cathedral, which is on Mott Street, in the city's oldest Little Italy, of why so many Italian women always wear black ("They are in perpetual mourning for our Lord"); and then returns at last to Side-Bet Benny, the lockjawed diner proprietor.

Only a few of the hundreds of people who know Gould have read any of the Oral History, and most of them take it for granted that it is gibberish. Those who make the attempt usually bog down after a couple of chapters and give up. Gould says he can count on one hand or on one foot those who have read enough of it to be qualified to form an opinion. One is Horace Gregory, the poet and critic. "I look upon Gould as a sort of Samuel Pepys of the Bowery," Gregory says. "I once waded through twenty-odd composition books, and most of what I saw had the quality of a competent high-school theme, but some of it was written with the clear and wonderful veracity of a child, and here and there were flashes of hard-bitten Yankee wit. If someone took the trouble to go through it and separate the good from the rubbish, as editors did with Thomas Wolfe's millions of words, it might be discovered that Gould actually has written a masterpiece." Another is E. E. Cummings, the poet, who is a close friend of Gould's. Cummings once wrote a poem about Gould, No. 261 in his "Collected Poems," which contains the following description of the history:

> . . . a myth is as good as a smile but little joe gould's quote oral
> history unquote might (publishers note) be entitled a wraith's
> progress or mainly awash while chiefly submerged or an amoral
> morality sort-of-aliveing by innumerable kind-of-deaths

Throughout the nineteen-twenties Gould haunted the office of the *Dial,* now dead, the most highbrow magazine of the time. Finally, in its April, 1929, issue, the *Dial* printed one of his shorter essays, "Civilization." In it he rambled along, jeering at the buying and selling of stocks as "a fuddy-duddy old maid's game" and referring to skyscrapers and steamships as "bric-a-brac" and giving his opinion that "the auto is unnecessary." "If all the perverted ingenuity which was put into making buzz-wagons had only gone into improving the breed of horses," he wrote, "humanity would be better off." This essay had a curious effect on American literature. A copy of the *Dial* in which it appeared turned up a few months later in a second-hand bookstore in Fresno, California, and was bought for a dime by William Saroyan, who then was twenty and floundering around, desperate to become a writer. He read Gould's essay and was deeply impressed and influenced by it. "It freed me from bothering about form," he says. Twelve years later, in the winter of 1941, in Don Freeman's studio on Columbus Circle, Saroyan saw some drawings Freeman had made of Gould for *Don Freeman's Newsstand,* a quarterly publication of pictures of odd New York scenes and personalities put out by the Associated American Artists. Saroyan became excited. He told Freeman about his indebtedness to Gould. "Who the hell is he, anyway?" Saroyan asked. "I've been trying to find out for years. Reading those few pages in the *Dial* was like going in the wrong direction and running into the right guy and then never seeing him again." Freeman told him about the Oral History. Saroyan sat down and wrote a commentary to accompany the drawings of Gould in *Newsstand*. "To this day," he wrote, in part, "I have not read anything else by Joe Gould. And yet to me he remains one of the few genuine and original American writers. He was easy and uncluttered, and almost all other American writing was uneasy and cluttered. It was not at home anywhere; it was trying too hard; it was miserable; it was a little sickly; it was literary; and it couldn't say anything simply. All other American writing was trying to get into one form or another, and no writer except Joe Gould seemed to have imagination enough to understand that if the worst came to the worst you didn't need to have any form at all. You didn't need to put what you had to say into a poem, an essay, a story, or a novel. All you had to do was say it." Not long after this issue of *Newsstand* came out, someone stopped Gould on Eighth Street and showed him Saroyan's endorsement of his work. Gould shrugged his shoulders. He had been on a spree and had lost his false teeth, and at the moment he was uninterested in literary matters. After thinking it over, however, he decided to call on Saroyan and ask him for help in getting some teeth. He found out somehow that Saroyan was living at the Hampshire House, on Central Park South. The doorman there followed Gould into the lobby and asked him what he wanted. Gould told him that he had come to see William Saroyan. "Do you know Mr. Saroyan?" the doorman asked. "Why, no," Gould said, "but that's all right. He's a disciple of mine." "What do you mean, disciple?" asked the doorman. "I mean," said Gould, "that he's a literary disciple of mine. I want to ask him to buy me some teeth." "Teeth?" asked the doorman. "What do you mean, teeth?" "I mean some store teeth," Gould said. "Some false teeth." "Come this way," said the doorman, gripping Gould's arm and ushering him to the street. Later Freeman arranged a meeting, and the pair spent several evenings together in bars. "Saroyan kept saying he wanted to hear all about the Oral History," Gould says, "but I never got a chance to tell him. He did all the talking. I couldn't get a word in edgewise."

As LONG AS HE can remember, Gould has been perplexed by his own personality. There are a number of autobiographical essays in the Oral History, and he says that all of them are attempts to explain himself to himself. In one, "Why I Am Unable To Adjust Myself To Civilization, Such As It Is, or Do, Don't, Do, Don't, A Hell Of A Note," he came to the conclusion that his shyness was responsible for everything. "I am introvert and extrovert all rolled in one," he wrote, "a warring mixture of the recluse and the Sixth Avenue auctioneer. One foot says do, the other says don't. One foot says shut your mouth, the other says bellow like a bull. I am painfully shy, but try not to let people know it. They would take advantage of me." Gould keeps his shyness well hidden. It is evident only when he is cold sober. In that state he is silent, suspicious, and constrained, but a couple of beers or a single jigger of gin will untie his tongue and put a leer on his face. He is extraordinarily responsive to alcohol. "On a hot night," he says, "I can walk up and down in front of a gin mill for ten minutes, breathing real deep, and get a jag on."

Even though Gould requires only a few drinks, getting them is sometimes quite a task. Most evenings he prowls around the saloons and dives on the west side of the Village, on the lookout for curiosity-seeking tourists from whom he can cadge beers, sandwiches, and small sums of money. If he is unable to find anyone approachable in the tumultuous saloons around Sheridan Square, he goes over to Sixth Avenue and works north, hitting the Jericho Tavern, the Village Square Bar & Grill, the Belmar, Goody's, and the Rochambeau. He has a routine. He doesn't enter a place unless it is crowded. After he is in, he bustles over to the telephone booth and pretends to look up a number.

While doing this, he scrutinizes the customers. If he sees a prospect, he goes over and says, "Let me introduce myself. The name is Joseph Ferdinand Gould, a graduate of Harvard, *magna cum difficultate,* class of 1911, and chairman of the board of Weal and Woe, Incorporated. In exchange for a drink, I'll recite a poem, deliver a lecture, argue a point, or take off my shoes and imitate a sea gull. I prefer gin, but beer will do." Gould is by no means a bum. He feels that the entertainment he provides is well worth whatever he is able to cadge. He doesn't fawn, and he is never grateful. If he is turned down politely, he shrugs his shoulders and leaves the place. However, if the prospect passes a remark like "Get out of here, you bum," Gould turns on him, no matter how big he is, and gives him a shrill, nasal, scurrilous tongue-lashing. He doesn't care what he says. When he loses his temper, he becomes fearless. He will drop his portfolio, put up his fists, and offer to fight men who could kill him with one halfhearted blow. If he doesn't find an audience on the trip up Sixth, he turns west on Eleventh and heads for the Village Vanguard, in a cellar on Seventh Avenue South. The Vanguard was once a sleazy rendezvous for arty people, but currently it is a thriving night club. Gould and the proprietor, a man named Max Gordon, have known each other for many years and are on fairly good terms much of the time. Gould always hits the Vanguard last. He is sure of it, and he keeps it in reserve. Since it became prosperous, the place annoys him. He goes down the stairs and says, "Hello, Max, you dirty capitalist. I want a bite to eat and a beer. If I don't get it, I'll walk right out on the dance floor and throw a fit." "Go argue with the cook," Gordon tells him. Gould goes into the kitchen, eats whatever the cook gives him, drinks a couple of beers, fills a bag with bread crumbs, and departs.

Despite his shyness, Gould has a great fondness for parties. There are many people in the Village who give big parties fairly often. Among them are a rich and idiosyncratic old doctor, a rich old spinster, a famous stage designer, a famous theatrical couple, and numbers of painters and sculptors and writers and editors and publishers. As often as not, when Gould finds out that any of these people are giving a party, he goes, and as often as not he is allowed to stay. Usually he keeps to himself for a while, uneasily smoking one cigarette after another and stiff as a board with tenseness. Sooner or later, however, impelled by a drink or two and by the desperation of the ill at ease, he begins to throw his weight around. He picks out the prettiest woman in the room, goes over, bows, and kisses her hand. He tells discreditable stories about himself. He becomes exuberant; suddenly, for no reason at all, he cackles with pleasure and jumps up and clicks his heels together. Presently he shouts, "All in favor of a one-man floor show, please say 'Aye'!" If he gets the slightest encouragement, he strips to the waist and does a hand-clapping, foot-stamping dance which he says he learned on a Chippewa reservation in North Dakota and which he calls the Joseph Ferdinand Gould Stomp. While dancing, he chants an old Salvation Army song, "There Are Flies on Me, There Are Flies on You, but There Are No Flies on Jesus." Then he imitates a sea gull. He pulls off his shoes and socks and takes awkward, headlong skips about the room, flapping his arms and letting out a piercing caw with every skip. As a child he had several pet gulls, and he still spends many Sundays on the end of a fishing pier at Sheepshead Bay observing gulls; he claims he has such a thorough understanding of their cawing that he can translate poetry into it. "I have translated a number of Henry Wadsworth Longfellow's poems into sea gull," he says.

Inevitably, at every party Gould goes to, he gets up on a chair or a table and delivers some lectures. These lectures are extracts from chapters of the Oral History. They are brief, but he gives them lengthy titles, such as "Drunk as a Skunk, or How I Measured the Heads of Fifteen Hundred Indians in Zero Weather" and "The Dread Tomato Habit, or Watch Out! Watch Out! Down with Dr. Gallup!" He is skeptical about statistics. In the latter lecture, using statistics he claims he found in financial sec-

tions in newspapers, he proves that "the eating of tomatoes by railroad engineers was responsible for fifty-three
per cent of the train wrecks in the United States during
the last seven years." When Gould arrives at a party, people who have never seen him before usually take one look
at him and edge away. Before the evening is over, however, a few of them almost always develop a kind of puzzled respect for him; they get him in a corner, ask him
questions, and try to determine what is wrong with him.
Gould enjoys this. "When you came over and kissed my
hand," a young woman told him one night, "I said to myself, 'What a nice old gentleman.' A minute later I looked
around and you were bouncing up and down with your
shirt off, imitating a wild Indian. I was shocked. Why do
you have to be such an exhibitionist?" "Madam," Gould
said, "it is the duty of the bohemian to make a spectacle of
himself. If my informality leads you to believe that I'm a
rum-dumb, or that I belong in Bellevue, hold fast to that
belief, hold fast, hold fast, and show your ignorance."

GOULD IS A NATIVE of Norwood, Massachusetts, a suburb of Boston. He comes from a family of physicians. His
grandfather, Joseph Ferdinand Gould, for whom he was
named, taught in the Harvard Medical School and had a
practice in Boston. His father, Clarke Storer Gould, was a

general practitioner in Norwood. He served as a captain in the Army Medical Corps and died of blood poisoning in a camp in Ohio during the First World War. The family was well-to-do until Gould was about grown, when his father invested unwisely in the stock of an Alaska land company. Gould says he went to Harvard only because it was a family custom. "I did not want to go," he wrote in one of his autobiographical essays. "It had been my plan to stay home and sit in a rocking chair on the back porch and brood." He says that he was an undistinguished student. Some of his classmates were Conrad Aiken, the poet; Howard Lindsay, the playwright and actor; Gluyas Williams, the cartoonist; and Richard F. Whitney, former president of the New York Stock Exchange. His best friends were three foreign students—a Chinese, a Siamese, and an Albanian.

Gould's mother had always taken it for granted that he would become a physician, but after getting his A.B. he told her he was through with formal education. She asked him what he intended to do. "I intend to stroll and ponder," he said. He passed most of the next three years strolling and pondering on the ranch of an uncle in Canada. In 1913, in an Albanian restaurant in Boston named the Scanderbeg, whose coffee he liked, he became acquainted with Theofan S. Noli, an archimandrite of the

Albanian Orthodox Church, who interested him in Balkan politics. In February, 1914, Gould startled his family by announcing that he planned to devote the rest of his life to collecting funds to free Albania. He founded an organization in Boston called the Friends of Albanian Independence, enrolled a score or so of dues-paying members, and began telegraphing and calling on bewildered newspaper editors in Boston and New York City, trying to persuade them to print long treatises on Albanian affairs written by Noli. After about eight months of this, Gould was sitting in the Scanderbeg one night, drinking coffee and listening to a group of Albanian factory workers argue in their native tongue about Balkan politics, when he suddenly came to the conclusion that he was about to have a nervous breakdown. "I began to twitch uncontrollably and see double," he says. From that night on his interest in Albania slackened.

After another period of strolling and pondering, Gould took up eugenics. He has forgotten exactly how this came about. In any case, he spent the summer of 1915 as a student in eugenical field work at the Eugenics Record Office at Cold Spring Harbor, Long Island. This organization, endowed by the Carnegie Institution, was engaged at that time in making studies of families of hereditary defectives, paupers, and town nuisances in several highly inbred communities. Such people were too prosaic for Gould; he decided to specialize in Indians. That winter he went out to North Dakota and measured the heads of a thousand Chippewas on the Turtle Mountain Reservation and of five hundred Mandans on the Fort Berthold Reservation. Nowadays, when Gould is asked why he took these measurements, he changes the subject, saying, "The whole matter is a deep scientific secret." He was happy in North Dakota. "It was the most rewarding period of my life," he says. "I'm a good horseman, if I do say so myself, and I like to dance and whoop, and the Indians seemed to enjoy having me around. I was afraid they'd think I was batty when I asked for permission to measure their noggins, but they didn't mind. It seemed to amuse them. Indians are the only true aristocrats I've ever known. They ought to run the country, and we ought to be put on the reservations." After seven months of reservation life, Gould ran out of money. He returned to Massachusetts and tried vainly to get funds for another head-measuring expedition. "At this juncture in my life," he says, "I decided to engage in literary work." He came to New York City and got a job as assistant Police Headquarters reporter for the *Evening Mail.* One morning in the summer of 1917, after he had been a reporter for about a year, he was basking in the sun on the back steps of Headquarters, trying to overcome a hangover, when the idea for the Oral History blossomed in his mind. He promptly quit his job and began writing. "Since that fateful morning," he once said, in a moment of exaltation, "the Oral History has been my rope and my scaffold, my bed and my board, my wife and my floozy, my wound and the salt on it, my whiskey and my aspirin, and my rock and my salvation. It is the only thing that matters a damn to me. All else is dross."

GOULD SAYS THAT HE RARELY has more than a dollar at any one time, and that he doesn't particularly care. "As a rule," he says, "I despise money." However, there is a widely held belief in the Village that he is rich and that he receives an income from inherited property in New England. "Only an old millionaire could afford to go around as shabby as you," a bartender told him recently. "You're one of those fellows that die in doorways and when the cops search them their pockets are just busting with bankbooks. If you wanted to, I bet you could step over to the West Side Savings Bank right this minute and draw out twenty thousand dollars." After the death of his mother in 1939, Gould did come into some money. Close friends of his say that it was less than a thousand dollars and that he spent it in less than a month, wildly buying drinks all over the Village for people he had never seen before. "He seemed miserable with money in his pockets," Gordon, the proprietor of the Vanguard, says. "When it was all gone, it seemed to take a load off his mind." While Gould was spending his inheritance, he did one thing that satisfied him deeply. He bought a big, shiny radio and took it out on Sixth Avenue and kicked it to pieces. He has never cared for the radio. "Five minutes of the idiot's babble that comes out of those machines," he says, "would turn the stomach of a goat."

During the twenties and the early thirties Gould occasionally interrupted his work on the Oral History to pose for classes at the Art Students' League and to do book-reviewing for newspapers and magazines. He says there were periods when he lived comfortably on the money he earned this way. Burton Rascoe, literary editor of the old *Tribune,* gave him a lot of work. In an entry in "A Bookman's Daybook," which is a diary of happenings in the New York literary world in the twenties, Rascoe told of an experience with Gould. "I once gave him a small book about the American Indians to review," Rascoe wrote, "and he brought me back enough manuscript to fill three complete editions of the Sunday *Tribune.* I especially honor him because, unlike most reviewers, he has never dogged me with inquiries as to why I never run it. He had his say, which was considerable, about the book, the author, and the subject, and there for him the matter ended." Gould says that he quit book-reviewing because he felt that it was beneath his dignity to compete with machines. "The Sunday *Times* and the Sunday *Herald Tribune* have machines that review books," he says. "You put a book in one of those machines and jerk down a couple of levers and a review drops out." In recent years Gould has got along on less than five dollars in actual money a week. He has a number of friends—Malcolm Cowley, the writer and editor; Aaron Siskind, the documentary photographer; Cummings, the poet; and Gordon, the night-club proprietor, are a few—who give him small sums of money regularly. No matter what they think of the Oral History, all these people have great respect for Gould's pertinacity.

GOULD HAS A POOR OPINION of most of the writers and poets and painters and sculptors in the Village, and doesn't mind saying so. Because of his outspokenness he has never been allowed to join any of the art, writing, cultural, or ism organizations. He has been trying for ten years to join the Raven Poetry Circle, which puts on the poetry exhibition in Washington Square each summer and is the most powerful organization of its kind in the Village, but he has been blackballed every time. The head of the Ravens is a retired New York Telephone Company employee named Francis Lambert McCrudden. For many years Mr. McCrudden was a collector of coins from coin telephones for the telephone company. He is a self-educated man and very idealistic. His favorite theme is the dignity of labor, and his major work is an autobiographical poem called "The Nickel Snatcher." "We let Mr. Gould attend our readings, and I wish we could let him join, but we simply can't," Mr. McCrudden once said. "He isn't serious about poetry. We serve wine at our readings, and that is the only reason he attends. He sometimes insists on reading foolish poems of his own, and it gets on your nerves. At our Religious Poetry Night he demanded permission to recite a poem he had written entitled 'My Religion.' I told him to go ahead, and this is what he recited:

> 'In winter I'm a Buddhist,
> And in summer I'm a nudist.'

And at our Nature Poetry Night he begged to recite a poem of his entitled 'The Sea Gull.' I gave him permission, and he jumped out of his chair and began to wave his arms and leap about and scream, 'Scree-eek! Scree-eek! Scree-eek!' It was upsetting. We are serious poets and we don't approve of that sort of behavior." In the summer of 1942 Gould picketed the Raven exhibition, which was held on the fence of a tennis court on Washington Square South. In one hand he carried his portfolio and in the other he held a placard on which he had printed: "JOSEPH

FERDINAND GOULD, HOT-SHOT POET FROM POETVILLE, A REFUGEE FROM THE RAVENS. POETS OF THE WORLD, IGNITE! YOU HAVE NOTHING TO LOSE BUT YOUR BRAINS!" Now and then, as he strutted back and forth, he would take a leap and then a skip and say to passers-by, "Would you like to hear what Joe Gould thinks of the world and all that's in it? Scree-eek! Scree-eek! Scree-eek!"

(1942)

Joe Gould's Secret

Joe Gould was an odd and penniless and unemployable little man who came to the city in 1916 and ducked and dodged and held on as hard as he could for over thirty-five years. He was a member of one of the oldest families in New England ("The Goulds were the Goulds," he used to say, "when the Cabots and the Lowells were clamdiggers"), he was born and brought up in a town near Boston in which his father was a leading citizen, and he went to Harvard, as did his father and grandfather before him, but he claimed that until he arrived in New York City he had always felt out of place. "In my home town," he once wrote, "I never felt at home. I stuck out. Even in my own home, I never felt at home. In New

York City, especially in Greenwich Village, down among the cranks and the misfits and the one-lungers and the has-beens and the might've-beens and the would-bes and the never-wills and the God-knows-whats, I have always felt at home."

Gould looked like a bum and lived like a bum. He wore castoff clothes, and he slept in flophouses or in the cheapest rooms in cheap hotels. Sometimes he slept in doorways. He spent most of his time hanging out in diners and cafeterias and barrooms in the Village or wandering around the streets or looking up friends and acquaintances all over town or sitting in public libraries scribbling in dime-store composition books. He was generally pretty dirty. He would often go for days without washing his face and hands, and he rarely had a shirt washed or a suit cleaned. As a rule, he wore a garment continuously until someone gave him a new one, whereupon he threw the old one away. He had his hair cut infrequently ("Every other Easter," he would say), and then in a barber college on the Bowery. He was a chronic sufferer from the highly contagious kind of conjunctivitis that is known as pinkeye. His voice was distractingly nasal. On occasion, he stole. He usually stole books from bookstores and sold them to secondhand bookstores, but if he was sufficiently hard pressed he stole from friends. (One terribly cold night, he knocked on the door of the studio of a sculptor who was almost as poor as he was, and the sculptor let him spend the night rolled up like a mummy in layers of newspapers and sculpture shrouds on the floor of the studio, and next morning he got up early and stole some of the sculptor's tools and pawned them.) In addition, he was nonsensical and bumptious and inquisitive and gossipy and mocking and sarcastic and scurrilous. All through the years, nevertheless, a long succession of men and women gave him old clothes and small sums of money and bought him meals and drinks and paid for his lodging and invited him to parties and to weekends in the country and helped him get such things as glasses and false teeth, or otherwise took an interest in him—some simply because they thought he was entertaining, some because they felt sorry for him, some because they regarded him sentimentally as a relic of the Village of their youth, some because they enjoyed looking down on him, some for reasons that they themselves probably weren't at all sure of, and some because they believed that a book he had been working on for many years might possibly turn out to be a good book, even a great one, and wanted to encourage him to continue working on it.

Gould called this book "An Oral History," sometimes adding "of Our Time." As he described it, the Oral History consisted of talk he had heard and had considered meaningful and had taken down, either verbatim or summarized—everything from a remark overheard in the street to the conversation of a roomful of people lasting for hours—and of essays commenting on this talk. Some talk has an obvious meaning and nothing more, he said, and some, often unbeknownst to the talker, has at least one other meaning and sometimes several other meanings lurking around inside its obvious meaning. The latter kind of talk, he said, was what he was collecting for the Oral History. He professed to believe that such talk might have great hidden historical significance. It might have portents in it, he said—portents of cataclysms, a kind of writing on the wall long before the kingdom falls—and he liked to quote a couplet from William Blake's "Auguries of Innocence":

> *The harlot's cry from street to street*
> *Shall weave Old England's winding-sheet.*

Everything depended, he said, on how talk was interpreted, and not everybody was able to interpret it. "Yes, you're right," he once said to a detractor of the Oral History. "It's only things I heard people say, but maybe I have a peculiar ability—maybe I can understand the significance of what people say, maybe I can read its inner meaning. *You* might listen to a conversation between two old men in a barroom or two old women on a park bench and think that it was the worst kind of bushwa, and *I* might listen to the same conversation and find deep historical meaning in it."

"In time to come," he said on another occasion, "people may read Gould's Oral History to see what went wrong with us, the way we read Gibbon's 'Decline and Fall' to see what went wrong with the Romans."

He told people he met in Village joints that the Oral History was already millions upon millions of words long and beyond any doubt the lengthiest unpublished literary work in existence but that it was nowhere near finished. He said that he didn't expect it to be published in his lifetime, publishers being what they were, as blind as bats, and he sometimes rummaged around in his pockets and brought out and read aloud a will he had made disposing of it. "As soon after my demise as is convenient for all concerned," he specified in the will, "my manuscript books shall be collected from the various and sundry places in which they are stored and put on the scales and weighed, and two-thirds of them by weight shall be given to the Harvard Library and the other third shall be given to the library of the Smithsonian Institution."

Gould almost always wrote in composition books—the kind that schoolchildren use, the kind that are ruled and spine-stitched and paper-bound and have the multiplication table printed on the back. Customarily, when he filled a book, he would leave it with the first person he met on his rounds whom he knew and trusted—the cashier of an eating place, the proprietor of a barroom, the clerk of a hotel or flophouse—and ask that it be put away and kept for him. Then, every few months, he would go from place to place and pick up all the books that had accumulated. He would say, if anyone became curious about this, that he was storing them in an old friend's house or in an old friend's apartment or in an old friend's studio. He hardly ever identified any of these old friends by name, although sometimes he would describe one briefly and vaguely—"a classmate of mine who lives in Connecticut and has a big attic in his house," he would say, or "a woman I know who lives alone in a duplex apartment," or "a sculptor I know who has a studio in a loft building." In talking about the Oral History, he always emphasized its length and its bulk. He kept people up to date on its length. One evening in June, 1942, for example, he told an acquaintance that at the moment the Oral History was "approximately nine million two hundred and fifty-five thousand words long, or," he added, throwing his head back proudly, "about a dozen times as long as the Bible."

In 1952, Gould collapsed on the street and was taken to Columbus Hospital. Columbus transferred him to Bellevue, and Bellevue transferred him to the Pilgrim State Hospital, in West Brentwood, Long Island. In 1957,

he died there, aged sixty-eight, of arteriosclerosis and senility. Directly after the funeral, friends of his in the Village began trying to find the manuscript of the Oral
History. After several days, they turned up three things
he had written—a poem, a fragment of an essay, and a
begging letter. In the next month or so, they found a few
more begging letters. From then on, they were unable to
find anything at all. They sought out and questioned
scores of people in whose keeping Gould might conceiv-
ably have left some of the composition books, and they
visited all the places he had lived in or hung out in that
they could remember or learn about, but without suc-
cess. Not a single one of the composition books was
found.

In 1942, for reasons that I will go into later, I became
involved in Gould's life, and I kept in touch with him during his last ten years in the city. I spent a good many hours
during those years listening to him. I listened to him when
he was sober and I listened to him when he was drunk. I
listened to him when he was cast down and meek—when,
as he used to say, he felt so low he had to reach up to touch
bottom—and I listened to him when he was in moods of
incoherent exaltation. I got so I could put two and two together and make at least a little sense out of what he was
saying even when he was very drunk or very exalted or in
both states at once, and gradually, without intending to, I

learned some things about him that he may not have wanted me to know, or, on the other hand, since his mind was circuitous and he loved wheels within wheels, that he may very well have wanted me to know—I'll never be sure. In any case, I am quite sure that I know why the manuscript of the Oral History has not been found.

When Gould died, I made a resolution to keep this as well as some of the other things I had inadvertently learned about him to myself—to do otherwise, it seemed to me at the time, would be disloyal; let the dead past bury its dead—but since then I have come to the conclusion that my resolution was pointless and that I should tell what I know, and I am going to do so.

Before I go any further, however, I feel compelled to explain how I came to this conclusion.

A few months ago, while trying to make some room in my office, I got out a collection of papers relating to Gould that filled half a drawer in a filing cabinet: notes I had made of conversations with him, letters from him and letters from others concerning him, copies of little magazines containing essays and poems by him, newspaper clippings about him, drawings and photographs of him, and so on. I had lost a good deal of my interest in Gould long before he reached Pilgrim State—as he grew older, his faults intensified, and even those who felt most kindly toward him and continued to see him got so they dreaded him—but as I went through the file folders, trying to decide what to save and what to throw out, my interest in him revived. I found twenty-nine letters, notes, and postal cards from him in the folders. I started out just glancing through them and ended up rereading them with care. One letter was of particular interest to me. It was dated February 12 or 17 or 19 (it was impossible to tell which), 1946; his handwriting had become trembly, and it always had been hard to read.

"I ran into a young painter I know and his wife in the Minetta Tavern last night," he wrote, "and they told me they had recently gone to a party in the studio of a woman painter named Alice Neel, who is an old friend of mine, and that during the evening Alice showed them a portrait of me she did some years ago. I asked them what they thought of it. The young painter's wife spoke first. 'It's one of the most shocking pictures I've ever seen,' she said. And he agreed with her. 'You can say that again,' he said. This pleased me very much, especially the young man's reaction, as he is a hot-shot abstractionist and way up front in the avant garde and isn't usually impressed by a painting unless it is totally meaningless and was completed about half an hour ago. I posed for this painting in 1933, and that was thirteen years ago, and the fact that people still find it shocking speaks well for it. Speaks well for the possibility that it may have some of the one quality that all great paintings have in common, the power to last. I may have written to you about this painting before, or talked about it, but I am not sure. If so, bear with me; my memory is going. There are quite a few paintings in studios around town that are well known to people in the art world but can't be exhibited in galleries or museums because they probably would be considered obscene and might get the gallery or museum in trouble, and this is one of them. Hundreds of people have seen it through the years, many of them painters who have expressed admiration for it, and I have a hunch that one of these days, the way people are growing accustomed to the so-called obscene, it will hang in the Whitney or the Metropolitan. Alice Neel comes from a small town near Philadelphia and went to the School of Design for Women in Philadelphia. She used to have a studio in the Village, but she moved uptown long ago. She is highly respected by many painters of her age and generation, although she is not too well known to the general public. She has work in important collections, but this may be her best work. Her best work, and it can't be shown in public. A kind of underground masterpiece. I wish sometime you'd go and see it. I'd be interested to know what you think. She doesn't show it to just anyone who asks, of course, but I will give you her telephone number and if you tell her I want you to see it I'm sure she will show it to you. . . ."

The day that I received this letter, I remembered, I had tried several times to call Miss Neel, but her telephone hadn't answered, and I had filed the letter away and Gould had never brought the matter up again and I had forgotten all about it. This day, on an impulse, I called Miss Neel and got her, and she said that of course I could see the Gould portrait, and gave me the address of her studio. The address turned out to be a tenement in a Negro and Puerto Rican neighborhood on the upper East Side, and Miss Neel turned out to be a stately, soft-spoken, good-looking blond woman in her middle fifties. Her studio was a floor-through flat on the third floor of the tenement. Against a wall in one room was a two-tiered rack filled with paintings resting on their sides. The Gould portrait, she said, was on the top tier. She had to stand on a chair and take out several other paintings in order to get at it. As she took them out, she held them up for me to see, and commented on them, and her comments were so offhand they sounded cryptic. One painting showed an elderly man lying in a coffin. "My father," she said. "Head clerk in the per-diem department." "Excuse me," I said, wondering what a per-diem department was but not really wanting to know, "the per-diem department of what?" "Excuse *me*," she said. "Pennsylvania Railroad in Philadelphia." Another was a painting of a young Puerto Rican man sitting up in a hospital bed and staring wide-eyed into the distance. "T.b.," she said. "Dying, but he didn't. Recovered and became a codeine addict." Another was a painting of a woman in childbirth. Then came a painting of a small, bearded, bony, gawky, round-shouldered man who was strip stark naked except for his glasses, and this was the portrait of Gould. It was a fairly large painting, and Gould seemed almost life-size in it. The background was vague; he appeared to be sitting on a wooden bench in a steam bath, waiting for the steam to come on. His bony hands were resting on his bony knees, and his ribs showed plainly. He had one set of male sexual organs in the proper place, another set was growing from where his navel should have been, and still another set was growing from the wooden bench. Anatomically, the painting was fanciful and grotesque but not particularly shocking; except for the plethora of sexual organs, it was a strict and sober study of an undernourished middle-aged man. It was the expression on Gould's face that was shocking. Occasionally, in one of his Village hangouts or at a party, Gould would become so full of himself that he would abruptly get to his feet and rush about the room, bowing to women of all ages and sizes and degrees of approachability, and begging them to dance with him, and sometimes attempting to embrace and kiss them. After a while, rebuffed on all sides, he would get tired of this. Then he would imitate the flight of a sea gull. He would hop and skip and leap and lurch about, flapping his arms up and down and cawing like a sea gull as he did so. "Scree-eek!" he would cry out. "I'm a sea gull." He would keep on doing this until people stopped looking at him and resumed their conversations. Then, to regain their attention, he would take off his jacket and shirt and throw them aside and do a noisy, hand-clapping, breast-beating, foot-stamping dance. "Quiet!" he would cry out. "I'm doing a dance. It's a sacred dance. It's an Indian dance. It's the full-moon dance of the Chippewas." His eyes would glitter, his lower jaw would hang loose like a dog's in midsummer and he would pant like a dog, and on his face would come a leering, gleeful, mawkishly abandoned expression, half satanic and half silly. Miss Neel had caught this expression. "Joe Gould was very proud of this picture and used to come and sit and look at it," Miss Neel said. She studied Gould's face with affection and amusement and also with what seemed to me to be a certain uneasiness. "I call it 'Joe Gould,' " she continued, "but I probably should call it 'A Portrait of an Exhibitionist.' " A few moments later, she added, "I don't mean to say that Joe was an exhibitionist. I'm sure he wasn't—technically. Still, to be perfectly honest, years ago, watching him at parties, I used to have a feeling that there was an old exhibitionist shut up inside him and trying to get out, like a spider shut up in a bottle. Deep down inside him. A frightful old exhibitionist—the kind you see late at night in the subway. And he didn't necessarily know it. That's why I painted him this way." I suddenly realized that in my mind I had replaced the real Joe Gould—or at least the Joe Gould I had known—with a cleaned-up Joe Gould, an after-death Joe Gould. By forgetting the discreditable or by slowly transforming the discreditable into the creditable, as one tends to do in thinking about the dead, I had, so to speak, respectabilized him. Now, looking at the shame-less face in the portrait, I got him back into proportion, and I concluded that if it was possible for the real Joe Gould to have any feeling about the matter one way or the other he wouldn't be in the least displeased if I told any-thing at all about him that I happened to know. Quite the contrary.

I FIRST SAW GOULD in the winter of 1932. At that time, I was a newspaper reporter, working mostly on crime news. Every now and then, I covered a story in Women's Court, which in those days was in Jefferson Market Court-house, at Sixth Avenue and Tenth Street, in Greenwich Village. In the block below the courthouse there was a Greek restaurant, named the Athens, that was a hangout for people who worked in the court or often had business in it. They usually sat at a long table up front, across from the cashier's desk, and Harry Panagakos, the proprietor, sometimes came over and sat with them. One afternoon, during a court recess, I was sitting at this table drinking coffee with Panagakos and a probation officer and a bail bondsman and a couple of Vice Squad detectives when a curious little man came in. He was around five feet four or five, and quite thin; he could hardly have weighed more than ninety pounds. He was bareheaded, and he carried his head cocked on one side, like an English sparrow. His hair was long, and he had a bushy beard. There were streaks of dirt on his forehead, obviously from rubbing it with dirty fingers. He was wearing an overcoat that was several sizes too large for him; it reached almost to the floor. He held his hands clasped together for warmth—it was a bitter-cold day—and the sleeves of the overcoat came down over them, forming a sort of muff. Despite his beard, the man, in the oversized overcoat, bareheaded and dirty-faced, had something childlike and lost about him: a child who had been up in the attic with other children trying on grownups' clothes and had become tired of the game and wandered off. He stood still for a few moments, getting his bearings, and then he came over to Panagakos and said, "Can I have something to eat now, Harry? I can't wait until tonight." At first Panagakos seemed annoyed, but then he shrugged his shoulders and told the man to go on back and sit down and he would step into the kitchen in a few minutes and

ask the chef to fix him something. Looking greatly relieved, the man walked hurriedly up the aisle between
two rows of tables. To be precise, he scurried up the aisle.
"Who in God's holy name is that?" asked one of the detectives. Panagakos said that the man was one of the Village bohemians. He said that the bohemians were
starving to death—in New York City, the winter of 1932
was the worst winter of the depression—and that he had
got in the habit of feeding some of them. He said that the
waiters set aside steaks and chops that people hadn't finished eating, and other pieces of food left on plates, and
wrapped them in wax paper and put them in paper bags
and saved them for the bohemians. Panagakos said that all
he asked was that they wait until just before closing time,
at midnight, to come in and collect the food, so the sight
of them trooping in and out wouldn't get on the nerves of
the paying customers. He said that he was going to give
this one some soup and a sandwich but that he'd have to
warn him not to come in early again. The detective asked
if the man was a poet or a painter. "I don't know what
you'd call him," Panagakos said. "His name is Joe Gould,
and he's supposed to be writing the longest book in the
history of the world."

Toward the end of the thirties, I quit my newspaper job
and went to work for *The New Yorker*. Around the same
time, I moved to the Village, and I began to see Gould fre-

quently. I would catch glimpses of him going into or coming out of one of the barrooms on lower Sixth Avenue—the Jericho Tavern or the Village Square Bar & Grill or the Belmar or Goody's or the Rochambeau. I would see him sitting scribbling at a table in the Jackson Square branch of the Public Library, or I would see him filling his fountain pen in the main Village post office—the one on Tenth Street—or I would see him sitting among the young mothers and the old alcoholics in the sooty, pigeony, crumb-besprinkled, newspaper-bestrewn, privet-choked, coffin-shaped little park at Sheridan Square. I worked a good deal at night at that time, and now and then, on my way home, around two or three in the morning, I would see him on Sixth Avenue or on a side street, hunched over and walking along slowly and appearing to be headed nowhere in particular, almost always alone, almost always carrying a bulging brown pasteboard portfolio, sometimes mumbling to himself. In my eyes, he was an ancient, enigmatic, spectral figure, a banished man. I never saw him without thinking of the Ancient Mariner or of the Wandering Jew or of the Flying Dutchman, or of a silent old man called Swamp Jackson who lived alone in a shack on the edge of a swamp near the small farming town in the South that I come from and wandered widely on foot on the back roads of the countryside at night, or of one of those men I used to puzzle over when I read the

Bible as a child, who, for transgressions that seemed mysterious to me, had been "cast out."

One morning in the summer of 1942, sitting in my office at *The New Yorker*, I thought of Gould—I had seen him on the street the night before—and it occurred to me that he might be a good subject for a Profile. According to some notes I made at the time—I made notes on practically everything I had to do with Gould, and I found these in the file drawer with the rest of the Gould memorabilia—it was the morning of June 10, 1942, a Wednesday morning. I happened to be free to start on something new, so I went in and spoke to one of the editors about the idea. I remember telling the editor that I thought Gould was a perfect example of a type of eccentric widespread in New York City, the solitary nocturnal wanderer, and that that was the aspect of him that interested me most, that and his Oral History, and not his bohemianism; in my time, I had interviewed a number of Greenwich Village bohemians and they had seemed to me to be surprisingly tiresome. The editor said to go ahead and try it.

I was afraid that I might have trouble persuading Gould to talk about himself—I really knew next to nothing about him, and had got the impression that he was austere and aloof—and I decided that I had better talk with some people who knew him, or were acquainted with him, at least, and see if I could find out the best way to approach him. I left the office around eleven and went down to the Village and began going into places along Sixth Avenue and bringing up Gould's name and getting into conversations about him with bartenders and waiters and with old-time Villagers they pointed out for me among their customers. In the middle of the afternoon, I telephoned the switchboard operator at the office and asked if there were any messages for me, as I customarily did when I was out, and she immediately switched me to the receptionist, who said that a man had been sitting in the reception room for an hour or so waiting for me to return. "I'll put him on the phone," she said. "Hello, this is Joe Gould," the man said. "I heard that you wanted to talk to me, so I dropped in, but the thing is, I'm supposed to go to the clinic at the Eye and Ear Infirmary, at Second Avenue and Thirteenth Street, and pick up a prescription for some eye trouble I've been having, and if it's one kind of prescription it won't cost anything but if it's another kind it may cost around two dollars, and I've just discovered that I don't have any money with me, and it's getting late, and I wonder if you'd ask your receptionist to lend me two dollars and you can pay her back when you come in and we can meet any time you say and have a talk and I'll pay you back then." The receptionist broke in and said that she would lend him the money, and then Gould came back on the phone and we agreed to meet at nine-thirty the next morning in a diner on Sixth Avenue, in the Village, called the Jefferson. He suggested both the time and the place.

When I got back to the office, I gave the receptionist her two dollars. "He was a terribly dirty little man, and terribly nosy," she said, "and I was glad to get him out of here." "What was he nosy about?" I asked. "Well, for one thing," she said, "he wanted to know how much I make. Also," she continued, handing me a folded slip of paper, "he gave me this note as he was leaving, and told me not to read it until he got on the elevator." "You have beautiful shoulders, my dear," the note said, "and I should like to kiss them." "He also left a note for you," she said, handing me another folded slip of paper. "On second thought," this note said, "nine-thirty is a little early for me. Let us make it eleven."

The Jefferson—it is gone now—was one of those big, roomy, jukeboxy diners. It was on the west side of Sixth Avenue, at the conjunction of Sixth Avenue, Greenwich Avenue, Village Square, and Eighth Street, which is the heart and hub of the Village. It stayed open all day and all night, and it was a popular meeting place. It had a long counter with a row of wobbly-seated stools, and it had a row of booths. When I entered it, at eleven, Gould was sitting on the first counter stool, facing the door and holding his greasy old pasteboard portfolio on his lap, and he looked the worst I had ever seen him. He was wearing a limp, dirty seersucker suit, a dirty Brooks Brothers button-down shirt with a frayed collar, and dirty sneakers. His face was greenish gray, and the right side of his mouth twitched involuntarily. His eyes were bloodshot. He was bald on top, but he had hair sticking out in every possible direction from the back and sides of his head. His beard was unkempt, and around his mouth cigarette smoke had stained it yellow. He had on a pair of glasses that were loose and lopsided, and they had slipped down near the end of his nose. As I came in, he lifted his head a little and looked at me, and his face was alert and on guard and yet so tired and so detached and so remotely reflective that it was almost impassive. Looking straight at me, he looked straight through me. I have seen the same deceptively blank expression on the faces of old freaks sitting on platforms in freak shows and on the faces of old apes in zoos on Sunday afternoons.

I went over and introduced myself to Gould, and he instantly drew himself up. "I understand you want to write something about me," he said, in a chipper, nasal voice, "and I greet you at the beginning of a great endeavor." Then, having said this, he seemed to falter and to lose confidence in himself. "I didn't get much sleep last night," he said. "I didn't get home. That is, I didn't get to the flophouse I've been staying in lately. I slept on the porch at St.

Joseph's R.C. until they opened the doors for the first Mass, and then I went in and sat in a pew until a few minutes ago." St. Joseph's, at Sixth Avenue and Washington Place, is the principal Roman Catholic church in the Village and one of the oldest churches in the city; it has two large, freestanding columns on its porch, behind which, shielded from the street, generations of unfortunates have slept. "I died and was buried and went to Hell two or three times this morning, sitting in that pew," Gould continued. "To be frank, I have a hangover and I'm broke and I'm terribly hungry, and I'd appreciate it very much if you'd buy me some breakfast."

"Of course," I said.

"Fried eggs on toast!" he called out commandingly to the counterman. "And let me have some coffee right away and some more with the eggs. Black coffee. And make sure it's hot." He slid off the stool. "If you're having something," he said to me, "call out your order, and let's sit in a booth. The waitress will bring it over."

WE TOOK A BOOTH, and the waitress brought Gould's coffee. It was in a thick white mug, diner style, and it was so hot it was steaming. Even so, tipping the mug slightly toward him without taking it off the table, he bent down and immediately began drinking it with little, cautious, quick, birdlike sips and gulps interspersed with little whimpering sounds indicating pleasure and relief, and almost at once color returned to his face and his eyes became brighter and his twitch disappeared. I had never before seen anyone react so quickly and so noticeably to coffee; brandy probably wouldn't have done any more for him, or cocaine, or an oxygen tent, or a blood transfusion. He drank the whole mug in this fashion, and then sat back and held his head on one side and looked me over.

"I suppose you're puzzled about me," he said. His tone of voice was condescending; he had got some of his confidence back. "If so," he continued, "the feeling is mutual, for I'm puzzled about myself, and have been since childhood. I seem to be a changeling or a throwback or a mutation of some sort in a highly respectable old New England family. Let me give you a few biographical facts. My full name is Joseph Ferdinand Gould, and I was named for my grandfather, who was a doctor. During the Civil War, he was surgeon of the Fourth Regiment, Massachusetts Volunteers, and later on he was a prominent obstetrician in Boston and taught in the Harvard Medical School. The Goulds, or my branch of them, have been in New England since the sixteen-thirties and have fought in every war in the history of the country, including King Philip's War and the Pequot War. We're related to many of the other early New England families, such as the Lawrences and the Clarkes and the Storers. My grandmother on my father's side was a direct descendant of John Lawrence, who arrived from England on the *Arbella* in 1630 and was the first Lawrence in this country, and she could trace her ancestry back to a knight named Robert Lawrence who lived in the twelfth century. She used to say that the Lawrence line, or this particular Lawrence line, was not only one of the oldest clearly traceable lines in New England but also one of the oldest clearly traceable lines in England itself, and that we should never forget it."

Gould abruptly began scratching himself. He went about it unself-consciously. He scratched the back of his neck, and then he thrust his hand inside his shirt and scratched his chest and ribs.

"I should've been born in Boston," he continued, "but I wasn't. My father, whose name was Clarke Storer Gould, was also a doctor. He was a Bostonian, but he had been prevailed upon to move out and practice in Norwood, Massachusetts, and he and my mother had been living there only a few months when I was born. Norwood is a fairly good-sized old Yankee town about fifteen miles southwest of Boston. It's a residential suburb, and it also has some printing plants and some sheepskin tanneries and an ink factory and a glue works. I was born at high noon on September 12, 1889, in a flat over Jim

Hartshorn's meat market. In Norwood, by the way, that's pronounced 'Jim Hatson.' A year or so later, my father built a big house on Washington Street, the main street of Norwood. Four-eighty-six Washington Street. It had three stories and twenty-one rooms, and it had gables and dormers and ornamental balconies and parquet floors, and it was one of the show places of Norwood. There was a mirror in our front hall that was eight feet high and decorated with gold cherubim. There were beautiful terra-cotta tiles around the fireplaces. There were diamond-shaped windows at the stair landings, and they had red, green, purple, and amber panes.

"As I said, my grandfather and my father were doctors, and when I was growing up I was well aware that my father hoped I would follow in his footsteps, just as he had followed in *his* father's footsteps. He never said so, but it was perfectly obvious to me and to everybody else that that was what he wanted. I loved my father, and I wanted him to think well of me, but I knew from the time I was a little boy and fainted at the sight of blood when I happened to see our cook wring the neck of a chicken that I was going to be a disappointment to him, because I really couldn't stand the idea of being a doctor; I kept it to myself, but that was the last thing in the world I wanted to be. Not that I had anything else in mind. The truth is, I wasn't much good at anything—at home or at school or at play. To begin with, I was undersized; I was a runt, a shrimp, a peanut, a half-pint, a tadpole. My nickname, when anybody thought to use it, was Pee Wee. Also, I was what my father called a catarrhal child—my nose ran constantly. Usually, when I was supposed to be paying attention to something, I was busy blowing my nose. Also, I was just generally inept. Not long ago, looking up something in the unabridged dictionary, I came across a word that sums up the way I was then, and, for that matter, the way I am now—'ambisinistrous,' or left-handed in both hands. My father didn't know what to make of me, and I sometimes caught him looking at me with a thoughtful expression on his face."

Gould stood up and took off his lopsided glasses and peered desperately at the counterman, who was evidently putting off starting on Gould's order until he had attended to everyone else in the diner, including some people who had come in after we had sat down, but the counterman deliberately ignored him and would not let him catch his eye.

"Anyhow," Gould went on, sitting back down resignedly, "when I was around thirteen, a couple of things happened that showed me pretty clearly where I stood in the world. At school, we used to do a lot of marching two by two. We'd march into assembly two by two, and we'd march out to recess two by two. I could never keep in step, so they used to put me on the end of the line and I'd bring up the rear, marching by myself. This particular day, I had been kept in after school, and the teacher had let me go to the library room to pick out a book to read, and I was alone in there and out of sight, squatting down at a bookcase in the back of the room trying to decide between two books, when the principal of the school, who was a man, came in with one of the men teachers, the math teacher. They each dumped some books down on the desk, and then they stood there for a few moments, talking about one thing and another, and all of a sudden I heard the principal say, 'Did you notice the Gould boy today?' The math teacher said something I didn't catch, and then the principal said, 'The disgusting little bastard can't even keep in step with himself.' The math teacher laughed and said something else I didn't catch, and then they went on out.

"Now, it so happened my father was on the school board and took a great interest in the school, and he and the principal saw quite a lot of each other. They were really very good friends; the principal and his wife used to come to our house for dinner, and my father and mother used to go to their house for dinner. Consequently, I was deeply shocked by the principal's remark. It hurt to over-hear myself being called a disgusting little bastard, but it was the disrespect to my father that hurt the most. 'The Gould boy'! That brought my father into it. If he had just said 'Joseph Gould,' it wouldn't've been so bad. It would've confined it to me. I felt that the principal had insulted my father. I felt that he had betrayed him. At the very least, he had made fun of him behind his back. In some strange way, it made me feel closer to my father than I had ever felt before, and it made me feel sorry for him—it made me want to make it up to him. So that night, after supper, I went into the parlor, where he was sitting reading, and I said to him, 'Father, I've been doing some thinking lately about what I'd like to be, and I've decided I'd like to study medicine and be a surgeon.' I thought it would please him twice as much if I said I wanted to be a surgeon. 'That'll be the day,' my father said. 'If you *did* become a surgeon, and if you performed operations the way you do everything else, when you got through with a patient you'd have his insides so balled up you'd have his heart hanging upside down and his liver turned around backward and his intestines wound around his lungs and his bladder joined on to his windpipe, and you'd have him walking on his hands and breathing through his behind and making water out of his left ear.' "

Gould sighed, and a look of intense sadness passed over

his face. "I held that remark against my father for a long time," he said. "Every once in a while, through the years, I'd remember it, and it would cut me to the quick. Then, years and years later, long after I had left home and long after my father had died, I was walking along the street one night here in New York and happened to think of it, and it must've been the first time I had ever thought of it objectively, for I suddenly burst out laughing."

At this moment, the waitress put a plate of fried eggs on toast and another mug of coffee in front of Gould. As soon as she turned her back, he took up a bottle of ketchup that was about half full, and emptied it on the plate, encircling the eggs with ketchup. Then he darted around to the next booth and brought back another bottle of ketchup, which was perhaps a third full, and emptied this on the plate also, completely covering eggs and toast. "I don't particularly like the confounded stuff," he said, "but I make it a practice to eat all I can get. It's the only grub I know of that's free of charge." He began eating, using a fork at first but quickly switching to a spoon. "Sometimes I go in a place and order a cup of tea," he said confidingly, "and I drink it and pay for it, and then I ask for a cup of hot water. The counterman thinks I'm going to make a second cup of tea with the same tea bag, which he doesn't mind: that's all right. Instead of which, I pour some ketchup in, and I have a very good cup of tomato bouillon free of charge.

Try it sometime." Gould finished his breakfast, and the waitress came to take away his plate. Catching sight of the empty ketchup bottles, she said, "You ought to have more self-respect than do a thing like that." "When I'm hungry, I don't have any self-respect," Gould said. "Anyhow, I didn't do it." He motioned with his head in my direction. "He did it," he said. "He turned both bottles up and drank them. You should've heard him. Glug, glug, glug! It was really quite embarrassing. Besides—and this is something you people can't seem to get through your heads—I'm not just an ordinary person. I'm Joe Gould—I'm Joe Gould, the poet; I'm Joe Gould, the historian; I'm Joe Gould, the wild Chippewa Indian dancer; and I'm Joe Gould, the greatest authority in the world on the language of the sea gull. I do you an honor by merely coming in here, and what do you do in return but bother me about such things as ketchup." This did not amuse the waitress. She was a portly, distracted, heavy-breathing woman, almost twice as big as Gould. "Who the hell do you think you are, you little rat?" she said. "One of these days, I'm going to pick you up by that Joe Gould beard of yours and throw you out of here." "Try it," said Gould, his voice becoming surprisingly intimidating, "and it'll be you and me all over the floor." He took a fistful of cigarette butts from a pocket of his seersucker jacket and put them on the table. As he did so, a shower of tobacco crumbs fell on his lap and on the floor and on the table, and I was afraid that he and the waitress would have some more words with each other. While she watched with disgust, Gould picked through the butts and chose one and fitted it in a long black cigarette holder. Paying no attention to the waitress, he lit it with an arch-elegant, Chaplinlike flourish, and she walked away.

"Now," he said, "to return to the story of my life for just a minute, I finished school in Norwood and then I went to Harvard. In 1911, I graduated from Harvard, and I spent the next few years debating in my mind what I should do next. By 1915, I had about given up hope of coming to any conclusion about this matter when I somehow became interested in the subject of eugenics. In fact, I became so interested that I borrowed some money from my mother and went to the Eugenics Record Office, at Cold Spring Harbor, Long Island, and took a summer course in eugenical field-work methods. After that, I decided I ought to put what I had learned to some use, and I borrowed a little more money from my mother and went out to North Dakota and began measuring the heads of Indians. In January and February, 1916, I measured the heads of five hundred Mandan Indians on the Fort Berthold Reservation, and in March and April I measured the heads of a thousand Chippewas on the Turtle Mountain Reservation, and then my money ran out. I wrote and asked my mother for more, and I received a telegram from her sending me my train fare and telling me to come home at once, which I did, whereupon she told me that she and my father were in financial difficulties to the point they had had to sell our house and were now renting it by the month from the new owner. It seems that some years previous to this my father had invested his own money as well as the money his family had left him in the stock of a company that had been formed to buy and develop a huge tract of land in Alaska. In other words, as smart as he was, my father had bought some gold-mine stock. And while I was out in North Dakota he and my mother had learned beyond all doubt that the stock was worthless.

"Well, I didn't see how I could be of any help to my parents, and I really had enjoyed measuring heads, so I went to Boston and called on various relatives and tried to raise money for another expedition to Indian reservations, but I was unsuccessful, to say the least. At this juncture in my life, my father took it upon himself to find a job for me. He had a friend in Boston, a Mr. Pickett, who was the lawyer for an estate that owned several rows of dwelling houses in Norwood. These houses were rented by the week to people who worked in the tanneries and the glue works, and Mr. Pickett offered me the job of collecting the rents. My father was tired of what he called my shilly-shallying, and I knew it was either take this job or leave

Norwood. I was terribly mixed up in my feelings about Norwood. I really never had felt at home in it, but there were things about it that I liked very much, or had liked at one time. I used to like to walk beside a little river that winds along the eastern and southern edges of it, the Neponset. And I used to like to wander around in a weedy old tumbledown New England graveyard that was directly in back of our house on Washington Street. The weeds were waist-high, and you could lie down and hide in them. You could hide in them and speculate on the rows upon rows of skeletons lying on their backs in the dirt down below. And I used to like some of the old buildings downtown, the old wooden stores. And I used to like the smell from the tanneries, particularly on damp mornings. It was a musky, vinegary, railroady smell. It was a mixture of the smells of raw sheepskins and oakbark acid that they used in the tanning vats and coal smoke, and it was a characteristic of the town. And I used to like a good many of the people—they had some old-Yankee something about them that appealed to me—but as I grew up I gradually realized that I was a kind of fool to them. I found out that even some of the dignified old men that I admired and respected the most made little jokes about me and laughed at me. I somehow just never fitted in. So, little by little, through the years, I had come to hate Norwood. I had come to hate it with all my heart and soul.

There were days, if wishes could kill, I would've killed every man, woman, and child in Norwood, including my mother and father. So I told my father that I couldn't accept Mr. Pickett's offer. 'I have decided,' I said, 'to go to New York and engage in literary work.' 'In that case, Son,' my father said, 'you've made your bed and you can lie in it.' I left Norwood a few days later. I left it with a light heart, even though I knew in my bones that I was leaving it for good, except I might possibly go back in the course of time for Christmas or summer vacations or such occasions as funerals—my father's funeral, my mother's funeral, my own funeral. I hadn't gone far, however, before I began having a reaction that took me by surprise. On the train, all the way to New York, I was so homesick for Norwood that I had to hold on to myself to keep from getting off and turning around and going back. Even today, I sometimes get really quite painfully homesick for Norwood. A sour smell that reminds me of the tanneries will bring it on, such as the smell from a basement down in the Italian part of the Village where some old Italian is making wine. That's one of the damnedest things I ever found out about human emotions and how treacherous they can be—the fact that you can hate a place with all your heart and soul and still be homesick for it. Not to speak of the fact that you can hate a person with all your heart and soul and still long for that person.

"I came to New York with the idea in mind of getting a job as a dramatic critic, for I thought that that would leave me time to write novels and plays and poems and songs and essays and an occasional scientific paper on some eugenical matter, and eventually I *did* succeed in getting a job as a sort of half messenger boy, half assistant Police Headquarters reporter for the *Evening Mail*. One morning in the summer of 1917, I was sitting in the sun on the back steps of Headquarters recovering from a hangover. In a second-hand bookstore, I had recently come across and looked through a little book of stories by William Carleton, the great Irish peasant writer, that was published in London in the eighties and had an introduction by William Butler Yeats, and a sentence in Yeats's introduction had stuck in my mind: 'The history of a nation is not in parliaments and battlefields, but in what the people say to each other on fair days and high days, and in how they farm, and quarrel, and go on pilgrimage.' All at once, the idea for the Oral History occurred to me: I would spend the rest of my life going about the city listening to people—eavesdropping, if necessary—and writing down whatever I heard them say that sounded revealing to me, no matter how boring or idiotic or vulgar or obscene it might sound to others. I could see the whole thing in my mind—long-winded conversations and short and snappy conversations, brilliant conversations and foolish conversations, curses, catch phrases, coarse remarks, snatches of quarrels, the mutterings of drunks and crazy people, the entreaties of beggars and bums, the propositions of prostitutes, the spiels of pitchmen and peddlers, the sermons of street preachers, shouts in the night, wild rumors, cries from the heart. I decided right then and there that I couldn't possibly continue to hold my job, because it would take up time that I should devote to the Oral History, and I resolved that I would never again accept regular employment unless I absolutely had to or starve but would cut my wants down to the bare bones and depend on friends and well-wishers to see me through. The idea for the Oral History occurred to me around half past ten. Around a quarter to eleven, I stood up and went to a telephone and quit my job."

A throbbing quality had come into Gould's voice.

"Since that fateful morning," he continued, squaring his shoulders and dilating his nostrils and lifting his chin, as if in heroic defiance, "the Oral History has been my rope and my scaffold, my bed and my board, my wife and my floozy, my wound and the salt on it, my whiskey and my aspirin, and my rock and my salvation. It is the only thing that matters a damn to me. All else is dross."

It was obvious that this was a set speech and that he had it down pat and that he had spoken it many times through the years and that he relished speaking it, and it made me obscurely uncomfortable.

"Just now, when you told the waitress that you were an authority on the language of the sea gull," I said, changing the subject, "did you mean it?"

Gould's face lit up. "When I was a child," he said, "my mother and I spent summers at a seaside town in Nova Scotia, a town called Clementsport, and every summer an old man would catch me a sea gull for a pet, and I sometimes used to have the impression that my sea gull was speaking to me, or trying to. Later on, when I was going to Harvard, I spent a great many Saturday afternoons sitting on T Wharf in Boston listening very carefully to sea gulls, and finally they got through to me, and little by little I learned the sea-gull language. I can understand it better than I can speak it, but I can speak it a lot better than you might think. In fact, I have translated a number of famous American poems into sea gull. Listen closely!"

He threw his head back and began to screech and chirp and croak and mew and squawk and gobble and cackle and caw, occasionally punctuating these noises with splutters. There was something singsong and sonorous in this racket that made it sound distantly familiar.

"Don't you recognize it?" cried Gould excitedly. "It's

'Hiawatha'! It's from the part called 'Hiawatha's Childhood.' Listen! I'll translate it back into English:

> *By the shores of Gitche Gumee,*
> *By the shining Big-Sea-Water,*
> *Stood the wigwam of Nokomis,*
> *Daughter of the Moon, Nokomis.*
> *Dark behind it rose the forest,*
> *Rose the black and gloomy pine-trees,*
> *Rose the firs with cones upon them . . ."*

Gould snickered; his spirits had risen the moment he had begun talking about sea gulls. "Henry Wadsworth Longfellow translates perfectly into sea gull," he said. "On the whole, to tell you the truth, I think he sounds better in sea gull than he does in English. And now, with your kind permission," he went on, standing up and starting to get out of the booth, a leering expression appearing on his face as he did so, "I'll step out in the aisle and give you my interpretation of a hungry sea gull circling above a fish pier where they're unloading fish." I had been aware, out of the corner of an eye, that the counterman had been watching us. Now this man spoke to Gould. "Sit down," he said. Gould whirled around and looked at the counterman, and I expected him to speak sharply to him, the way he had spoken to the waitress. He surprised me. He sat down meekly and obediently, without opening his mouth. Then, picking up his portfolio and putting it under his arm, as if preparing to go, he leaned across the table and began talking to me in a low voice. "You know the money I borrowed from you yesterday to get the eye prescription," he said. "Well, I started over to the Eye and Ear Infirmary, but on the way something came up, and when I got there the clinic was closed, and I'm in a worse fix today than yesterday as far as money is concerned, and the clinic closes earlier on Thursdays than on Wednesdays, and I wonder if you could lend me two or three or four or maybe five dollars, so I can go get the prescription and start using it. We can continue our talk some other time."

"Of course," I said.

"You won't mind?"

"Oh, no," I said. "Except I was hoping I could see some of the Oral History and maybe read some of it."

"I can easily arrange that," Gould said.

He sat his portfolio on his lap and untied it and opened it and dug around in it and brought out two composition books and put them on the table. "You'll find a chapter of the Oral History in each of these," he said. "I finished them only night before last. I've still got to polish them up a little, but you won't have any trouble reading them." He kept on digging around in the portfolio, using both hands. "In the twenties and thirties, a few bits and pieces and fragments of the Oral History were published in little

magazines," he said, "and I have copies of them somewhere in here." He took a small, rolled-up paper bag with
a rubber band around it from the deepest part of the portfolio and looked at it inquisitively. "What in hell is this?"
he said, opening the bag and peering into it. "Oh, yes," he
said. "Cigarette butts." He carefully put the bag back in
the portfolio. "Sometimes, in wet weather or snow all over
the streets," he said, "it's good to have some butts stuck
away." Then he brought out four magazines one by one
and stacked them on the table. They were dog-eared and
grease-spotted and coffee-stained.

"Here's Ezra Pound's old magazine the *Exile,*" he said,
riffling the pages of the one on top. "The *Exile* lasted exactly four issues, and this is the second issue—Autumn,
1927—and there's a chapter from the Oral History in it. I
have E. E. Cummings to thank for that. Cummings is one
of my oldest friends in New York. He and I come from
pretty much the same kind of New England background,
and our years at Harvard overlapped—my last year was his
first year—but I got to know him in the Village. Sometime
around 1923 or '24 or '25, Cummings spoke to Pound
about me and the Oral History, and then Pound wrote to
me, and we got into a correspondence that extended over
several years. Pound became very enthusiastic about my
plan for the History. He printed this little selection in the
Exile, and later on, in his book 'Polite Essays,' after speak-

ing of William Carlos Williams as a great, neglected American writer, he referred to me as 'that still more unreceived and uncomprehended native hickory, Mr. Joseph Gould.' And here's *Broom* for August–November 1923. It has a chapter from the History—Chapter C-C-C-L-X-V-I-I-I. At that time I was numbering the chapters with Roman numbers. And here's *Pagany* for April–June, 1931. It has some snippets from the History.

"And here's the greatest triumph of my life so far—the *Dial* for April, 1929. There are two essays from the Oral History in it. Marianne Moore, the poet, was editor of the *Dial*, and her office was right down here in the Village— on Thirteenth Street, just east of Seventh Avenue. It was one of those old houses—red brick, three stories high, a steep stoop leading up to the parlor floor, an ailanthus tree growing at a slant in front—that have always typified the Village to me. I used to drop in there about once a week and sit in her outer office all morning and sometimes all afternoon, too, reading back copies, and whenever I was able to wangle a little time with her I would try to get her to see the literary importance of the Oral History, and finally she printed these two little essays. Everything else I've ever done may disappear, but I'll still be immortal, just because of them. The *Dial* was the greatest literary magazine ever published in this country. It published a great many masterpieces and near-masterpieces as well as a great many curiosities and monstrosities, and there'll be bound volumes of it in active use in the principal libraries of the world as long as the English language is spoken and read. 'The Waste Land' came out in it. So did 'The Hollow Men.' Eliot reviewed 'Ulysses' for it. Two great stories by Thomas Mann came out in it—'Death in Venice' and 'Disorder and Early Sorrow.' Pound's 'Hugh Selwyn Mauberley' came out in it, and so did Hart Crane's 'To Brooklyn Bridge,' and so did Sherwood Anderson's 'I'm a Fool.' Joseph Conrad wrote for it, and so did Joyce and Yeats and Proust, and so did Cummings and Gertrude Stein and Virginia Woolf and Pirandello and George Moore and Spengler and Schnitzler and Santayana and Gorki and Hamsun and Stefan Zweig and Djuna Barnes and Ford Madox Ford and Miguel de Unamuno and H. D. and Katherine Mansfield, and a hundred others. For centuries to come, people will be going through the bound volumes looking up things by those writers, and now and then one of them will surely notice my two little essays and become curious about them and read them (God knows they aren't very long), and that's closer to immortality than a good many of my rooting and tooting contemporaries are likely to get—best-sellers, interviews on the radio, the dry little details of their dry little lives in *Who's Who,* photographs of their empty faces in the book-review sections, six or seven divorced wives, and all. Just look at some of the other things in this issue. A poem by Hart Crane. An essay by Logan Pearsall Smith. A couple of photographs of a sculpture of a nude by Maillol. A Paris Letter by Paul Morand. A piece about the theatre by Padraic Colum. A book review by Bertrand Russell."

Gould pushed the magazines and the composition books across the table to me. "Take them along and read them," he said.

Outside the diner, on the sidewalk, we agreed to meet again on Saturday night. "But not in the diner," Gould said. "I used to get along very well with the countermen and the waitresses in there. They used to kid around with me and I used to kid around with them. But they seem to have turned against me." A deeply troubled look appeared on his face, a haunted look, and he was silent for a few moments, reflecting. Then he shrugged his shoulders, as if dismissing the matter from his mind, but evidently the matter would not stay dismissed, for right away he started talking about it again. "In recent years," he said, "quite a few people have turned against me. Men and women all over the Village who once were good friends of mine now hate me and loathe me and despise me. You're bound to run into some of them, and they'll probably give you various reasons why they feel that way, and I guess I ought to get in ahead of them and give you the real reason. Would you like to hear it?"

I said that I would.

"The real reason," he said, "is a certain poem I wrote."

We walked slowly along Sixth Avenue.

"In the early thirties, because of the depression," he went on, "a good many people in the Village got interested in Marxism and became radicals. All of a sudden, most of the poets down here became proletarian poets and most of the novelists became proletarian novelists and most of the painters became proletarian painters. I know a woman who's married to a rich doctor and collects art and has a daughter who's a ballet dancer, and I ran into her one day and she informed me very proudly that her daughter was now a proletarian ballet dancer. The trouble is, the more radical these people became, the more know-it-all they became. And the more self-important. And the more self-satisfied. They sat around in the same old Village hang-outs that they had sat around in when they were just ordinary bohemians and they talked as much as they ever had, only now it wasn't art or sex or booze that they talked about but the coming revolution and dialectical material-ism and the dictatorship of the proletariat and what Lenin meant when he said this and what Trotsky meant when he said that, and they acted as if any conclusions they arrived at on these matters might have a far-reaching effect on the future of the whole world. In other words, they com-pletely lost their sense of humor. The way they talked about the proletariat, you'd think they were all the sons and daughters of iron puddlers, but the truth was, a surprisingly large number of them came from families that were either middle-class or upper-class and either very well-to-do or really quite rich. As time went on, I began to feel like a stranger among them. It wasn't so much their politics that bothered me, beyond the fact that politics of any kind bores the living hell out of me; it was the self-important way they talked about politics. As much as anything else, it was the way they said 'we.' Instead of '*I* think this' or '*I* think that,' it was always '*We* think this' or '*We* think that.' I couldn't get used to the 'we.' I began to feel intimidated by it. Once, trying to make a joke and lighten the atmosphere, I blurted out to one of them that I belonged to a party that had only one member and the name of it was the Joe Gould Party. He said that every time I made such remarks and joked about serious matters I showed myself in my true colors. 'We're on to you and people like you,' he said. 'When you act the clown, all you're doing is trying to hide the fact that you're a reactionary. To be frank about it,' he said, 'we would classify you as a parasite, a reactionary parasite. As for the Oral History,' he said, 'all you're doing in that, as far as we're concerned, is collecting the verbal garbage of the bourgeoisie.'

"At that time, in the summer, one of the novelties of

the Village was the sidewalk café in front of the Brevoort Hotel, at Fifth Avenue and Eighth Street. It was just a couple of rows of tables set back behind a hedge growing in a row of wooden boxes painted white, but people thought it was very European and very elegant. For some reason, this café was a great gathering place for the Village radicals. One afternoon in the summer of 1935, I was walking past it and I didn't have a penny in my pocket and I was hungry—not just a little hungry, the way I usually am, but so hungry I was dizzy and my eyes wouldn't focus right and my gums were sore and I had a sick headache and a dull, gnawing pain in the pit of my stomach—and a number of them were sitting there drinking the best Martinis money could buy and eating good French cooking and gravely discussing some matter no doubt having to do with the coming revolution, when a poem popped into my mind. I called it 'The Barricades.' That night, at a Village party, I stood up and said I had a proletarian poem I wanted to recite, and I recited this poem. It really wasn't much of a poem—in fact, it was just a piece of doggerel—but a surprising thing happened. Some of the people were mildly amused by it and laughed a little, which was all I had expected and all I had wanted, but there were several Village radicals and radical sympathizers present, including the man who had let me in on the fact that I was a reactionary parasite, and they were shocked. At first, I thought they were kidding me, pulling my leg, but they weren't, they were genuinely shocked—they looked at me the way deeply religious people might look at someone who had done something horribly sacrilegious—and when they got over their shock they became angry. They became so angry and hysterical that I left the party, which was away over on the east side of the Village, and started walking back to the west side. On Ninth Street, near University Place, I looked in the window of a restaurant called Aunt Clemmy's and saw a miscellaneous group of Villagers sitting around a table in there, some of whom I vaguely knew, and I decided to try 'The Barricades' out on them. I went in and recited it to them, and the same thing happened—some laughed politely and some got blazing mad. Then I went into a real old-time Village restaurant on Eighth Street, called Alice McCollister's—the kind of place that has red water glasses—and recited it to some people in there, and the same thing happened. Then I went over to Sheridan Square and went into a cafeteria that was the most popular late-at-night bohemian hangout in the Village at the time, a Stewart's cafeteria, and recited it in there, and the same thing happened. I was amazed at the fanatical reaction some people had to the poem. They practically foamed at the mouth. At the same time, I was delighted. I began to spend a good many evenings just going around the Village looking for opportunities to recite 'The Barricades.' Pretty soon, I found a way to make it even more inflammatory. Instead of reciting it, I would work myself into a state and chant it. I would chant it in a highly excited voice, the voice of a flaming revolutionary, and shake my fist at the end of each line. It got so, in some places in the Village, late at night, all I had to do was stand up and say that I had a proletarian poem I wanted to recite and half the people would leap to their feet and try to stop me and the other half would leap to their feet and egg me on.

"I go to as many Village parties as I can. I go for the free food and liquor and for material for the Oral History. I'm invited to some, and I hear about others on the Village grapevine and just go. One Saturday night a few months after I wrote 'The Barricades,' I showed up at a big party in a studio on Washington Square South. I hadn't been invited, but I knew the man and his wife who were giving it, and I had been going uninvited to their parties for years. When I rang the bell, the wife came to the door, and it didn't seem to me that she was as friendly as she had been in times gone by, but she asked me to come in. I went over and sat in a corner and had a number of drinks, after which it occurred to me that I should create a little diversion and repay my hosts by singing a song, so I stood up and announced that I had a proletarian poem I wanted to recite. Everybody suddenly became quiet, and I took a quick look around the room. It was a big room and there were a lot of people in it, and every face I looked at looked back at me with hatred. That didn't particularly disturb me. I'm used to that. Then I took a closer look around, and here and there, in among the faces of total strangers and the faces of people whom I knew but who meant nothing to me, I saw the faces of several men and women who had always been ready and willing to give me a little money or stake me to a meal or help me out in various other ways, and their faces were as cold and hostile as the others. And that *did* disturb me. That sobered me up immediately. I suddenly woke up to the fact that without quite realizing what I was doing I had made God only knows how many enemies. Since then, I've been trying to repair the damage, but it doesn't do any good. I never recite 'The Barricades' in public anymore—oh, I do if I'm sure of my audience—and quite a lot of time has gone by, but the Village radicals haven't forgiven me. They cut me dead on the street. If a group of them are sitting in a cafeteria and I sit down near them, they move away. If I stand near them at a bar, they move away. Some of them used to welcome me when I showed up at parties at their places, but now they shut the door in my face. And I've found out that every time my name comes up in conversation they revile me and disparage me and vilify me. And the worst thing is, they communicate the way they feel about me to others. Sooner or later, they'll turn everybody in the Village against me. The countermen and the waitresses in the diner, for example—I'm sure they've turned against me simply because they've heard some of the Village radicals making remarks about me and running me down. Oh, well, what's done's done. Here," he said, handing me his portfolio, "hold this, and I'll recite 'The Barricades' for you."

He straightened his tie and buttoned his dirty seersucker jacket. He drew himself excessively erect, like a schoolboy pledging allegiance to the flag. Then, raising his right fist in the air, he recited the following poem:

> *"This prissy hedge in front of the Brevoort*
> *Is but a symbol of the coming revolution.*
> *These are the barricades,*
>   *The barricades,*
>   *The barricades.*
> *And behind these barricades,*
>   *Behind these barricades,*
>   *Behind these barricades,*
> *The Comrades die!*
>   *The Comrades die!*
>   *The Comrades die!*
> *And behind these barricades,*
>   *The Comrades die—*
>   *Of overeating."*

Gould took back his portfolio. "On the other hand," he said, "as far as the people in the diner are concerned, it may not be that at all. I've been terribly run down and nervous this summer, and when I get that way, I scratch a lot. It's just a nervous habit—I've been doing it since childhood. The people in the diner have undoubtedly noticed me scratching, and they may have gotten it in their heads that I'm lousy, and *that* may very well be why they've turned against me." He had been speaking calmly, but now his manner changed. His face was abruptly contorted by an expression of pain and fury, and he spat on the street. "The absolutely hideous and disgusting and unspeakable God-damned truth of the matter is," he said, "I *am* lousy. I discovered it this morning while I was sitting through all those Masses in St. Joseph's. It's the second time in a month. I'll have to go to the Municipal Lodging House tonight and take a bath and let them put my clothes in the fumigator." He shook his head, vaguely. "This is no way to live," he said—and his voice sounded defeated—"but it's the only way I *can* live and work on the Oral History."

I started to try to say something optimistic but sensed that I ran the risk of being presumptuous; a man who has no lice on him is not in a very good position to minimize the disagreeableness of lice if he is talking to a man who is crawling with them, so I changed the subject to where we should meet on Saturday night. We decided that we would meet in Goody's, one of the saloons on Sixth Av enue in the Village. Then we said goodbye, and Gould started across the street. After he had gone a few steps, he suddenly did an about-face and hurried back to me.

"I just remembered something else I want to tell you," he said. "Something about the *Dial*. For a magazine of its kind, the *Dial* had a long life. It lasted nine and a half years. As I told you, the issue that has my contribution in it—the one I just gave you—was the issue for April, 1929. It lasted only three more issues. After the July issue, it discontinued publication, and that was a great shock to everyone who had any interest whatsoever in the cultural life of this country. In the Village, about the only thing people wanted to talk about for weeks was *who* killed the *Dial* or *what* killed the *Dial*. I wrote a poem about this."

Gould drew himself erect, as he had done before, and recited this poem:

> " 'Who killed the Dial?'
> 'Who killed the Dial?'
> 'I,' said Joe Gould,
> 'With my inimitable style,
> I killed the Dial.' "

As he recited it, he watched my face. When he finished it, I laughed more than he had expected me to, I think, and I was struck by how much pleasure this gave him. His bloodshot little eyes glowed with pleasure. Then, giggling, he hurried off.

IT WAS A CLOUDY DAY and looked as if it might pour down any minute, but I disregarded the weather and went over and sat on a bench under the big old elm in the northwest corner of Washington Square and opened one of Gould's composition books. On the first page was carefully lettered, "DEATH OF DR. CLARKE STORER GOULD. A CHAPTER OF JOE GOULD'S ORAL HISTORY." The chapter was divided into an introduction and four sections. The sections were headed: "FINAL ILLNESS," "DEATH," "FUNERAL," and "CREMATION." "The first thing I must deal with in this account of my father's death," Gould wrote in his introduction, "is that, for me, he died twice. In the summer of 1918, I left New York City, where I was getting down to work in earnest on the Oral History, and went up to Norwood to spend a month with my mother. The first World War was going on at that time, and my father was serving as a captain in the Medical Corps of the United States Army and was stationed at Camp Sherman, Chillicothe, Ohio. He was assistant adjutant of the base hospital. The second afternoon I was home, my mother went to the nearby town of Dedham to visit a friend, and I took a walk downtown, to the business district of Norwood. While we were both absent from the house, a doctor in Boston who was a friend of my father's telephoned my mother, and our cook, an old German woman who didn't understand English any too well and wasn't any too bright to begin with, took the call. The doctor in Boston said he was calling to ask my mother to inform my father the next time she wrote to him that another Boston doctor who was also a friend of my father's and had in fact been stationed with him for a while at Camp Sherman had died that day of blood poisoning in another camp out in the Middle West, but the old cook got it all balled up and understood him to say that my father had died that day of blood poisoning out at Camp Sherman. When I came home in the middle of the afternoon, she was sitting in the kitchen crying, and she told me that my father was dead. I went upstairs to my room and drew the shades and sat there mourning my father. I was overwhelmed with grief. Late in the afternoon my mother came home and immediately got on the telephone and called the doctor in Boston and ascertained what he had really told the cook. And then a curious thing happened to me—even though, intellectually, I knew that my father was not dead, I could not stop mourning him. For me, the blow had fallen. I sank into a mood of deep sorrow and could not rouse myself from it. I mourned my father all the rest of my visit to Norwood, and I continued to mourn him for several weeks after returning to New

York City. My father was honorably discharged from the Army on December 28, 1918, and returned at once to Norwood and resumed his practice. After he had been back in Norwood for less than three months, he became seriously ill and was taken to the Peter Bent Brigham Hospital in Boston, where he died early in the A.M. of Friday, March 28, 1919, aged fifty-four. And now I must put down the fact that his illness was septicemia, or blood poisoning, which was and is to me an astonishing coincidence. When I received the news of his death, I did not mourn him at all. As far as I was concerned, he was already dead. When I write my autobiography, I am going to make the flat statement in it that my father died of blood poisoning in an Army camp in Ohio during the first World War, and I am going to insist that this be so stated in any biographical material that is written about me as long as I am alive and have any control over such things, for to me my father's untrue death was his true death. I have no misgivings about this. In autobiography and biography, as in history, I have discovered, there are occasions when the facts do not tell the truth. However, in this account, I am going to deal only with what was, I must admit, my father's actual and factual death."

Gould's writing was very much like his conversation; it was a little stiff and stilted and mostly rather dull, but enlivened now and then by a surprising observation or bit of information or by sarcasm or malice or nonsense. It was full of digressions; there were digressions that led to other digressions, and there were digressions within digressions. Gould's father had belonged to the Universalist Church and the Masons, and his funeral service had been conducted jointly by the pastor of the local Universalist church and the chaplain and the Worshipful Master of the local Masonic lodge. Gould described the Universalist part of the service, and went from that to a discussion of the subtle differences between the members of the Universalist, Unitarian, and Congregational churches in New England towns, and went from that to a discussion of the differences between an Easter service he had once attended in an Albanian Orthodox Catholic church in Boston with a friend of his, an Albanian student at Harvard, and Easter services he had attended in Roman Catholic churches, and went from that to a description of a strange but unusually good meat stew he had once eaten in a basement restaurant in Boston frequented by Albanian shoe-factory workers that the Albanian student had taken him to ("They said it was lamb and it may have been mutton," he wrote, "but it was probably goat, either that or horse meat, not that I have any objection to goat meat or horse meat, having had the experience of eating boiled dog with the Chippewa Indians, which incidentally tasted like mutton, only sweeter, although I should point out here that eating dog has a ceremonial significance to the Chippewas and might be compared to our communion services and consequently the taste per se is not of great importance"), and went from that to a description of a baked-bean pot he had once seen in the window of an antique store on Madison Avenue that was exactly like the baked-bean pot used in the kitchen of his home in Norwood when he was a child. "Gazing at that so-called ANTIQUE baked-bean pot," he wrote, "I felt for the first time that I understood something about Time." He then began a description of the Masonic part of his father's funeral service, but went astray almost immediately with a digression on the importance of the Masons and the Elks and the Woodmen of the World and similar fraternal orders in the night life of small towns, which he interrupted at one point for a subsidiary digression on the subject of life insurance. "I wonder what Lewis and Clark would have thought of life insurance," he wrote in the course of the latter digression, "never mind Daniel Boone." (He had run a line through "never mind" and had written "let alone" just above it; then he had run a line through "let alone" and had written "not to speak of" just above *it;* then he had run a line through "not to speak of"; and then, in the margin, beside "never mind," he had written "stet.") Scattered throughout the book were many sentences that were wholly irrelevant; they seemed to be thoughts that had popped into his mind as he wrote, and that he had put down at once, because he didn't want to forget them. In the description of the Easter service in the Albanian church, for example, apropos of nothing that went before or came after, was this sentence: "Mr. Osgood, the Indian teacher at Armstrong, N.D., said that whiskey made the Sioux murderous and the Chippewa good-natured."

On the cover of the other composition book was lettered, "THE DREAD TOMATO HABIT, A CHAPTER OF JOE GOULD'S ORAL HISTORY." I couldn't make much sense out of this chapter until I skipped around in it and found that it was mock-serious and that its purpose was to make fun of statistics. Gould maintained that a mysterious disease was sweeping the country. "It is so mysterious that doctors are unaware of its existence," he wrote. "Furthermore, they do not want to become aware of its existence because it is responsible for a high percentage of the human misfortunes ranging from acne to automobile accidents and from colds to crime waves that they blame directly or indirectly on microbes or viruses or allergies or neuroses or psychoses and get rich by doing so." Gould devoted several pages to a description of the nature of the disease, and then stated that he knew the cause of it and was the only one who did. "It is caused by the increased consumption of tomatoes both raw and cooked and in the form of soup, sauce, juice, and ketchup," he wrote, "and therefore I have named it solanacomania. I base this name on *Solanaceae*, the botanical name for the dreadful nightshade family, to which the tomato belongs." At this point, Gould began filling page after page with unrelated statistics that he had obviously copied out of the financial and business sections of newspapers. "If this be true," he wrote after each statistic, "this also must be true," and then he introduced another statistic. He filled twenty-eight pages with these statistics. "And now," he wrote, winding up the chapter, "I hope I have proven, and I have certainly done so to my own satisfaction, that the eating of tomatoes by railroad engineers was responsible for fifty-three per cent of the train wrecks in the United States during the last seven years."

I was puzzled. These chapters of the Oral History bore no relation at all that I could see to the Oral History as Gould had described it. There was no talk or conversation in them, and unless they were looked upon as monologues by Gould himself there was nothing oral about them. I turned to the little magazines Gould had given me, and found that his contributions to them were brief but rambling essays, each of which had a one- or two-word title and a subtitle stating that it was "a chapter of" or "a selection from" the Oral History. In the *Exile*, his subject was "Art." In *Broom*, his subject was "Social Position." He had two essays in the *Dial*—"Marriage" and "Civilization."

And he had two in *Pagany*—"Insanity" and "Freedom."
By this time, I had read enough of Gould's writing to
know what these essays were. They were digressions cut
out of chapters of the Oral History by the editors of the little magazines or by Gould himself and given titles of their
own. In other words, they were more of the same. I read
them without much interest until, in the "Insanity" essay,
I came across three sentences that stood out sharply from
the rest. These sentences were plainly meant by Gould to
be a sort of poker-faced display of conceit, but it seemed
to me that he told more in them than he had intended to.
In the years to come, as I got to know him better, they
would return to my mind a great many times. They appeared at the end of a paragraph in which he had made
the point that he was dubious about the possibility of di-
viding people into sane and insane. "I would judge the
sanest man to be him who most firmly realizes the tragic
isolation of humanity and pursues his essential purposes
calmly," he wrote. "I suppose I feel about it in this way because I have a delusion of grandeur. I believe myself to be
Joe Gould."

ON SATURDAY NIGHT, June 13, 1942, I went into
Goody's to keep the appointment I had made with Gould.
Goody's (the proprietor's name was Goodman) was on
Sixth Avenue, between Ninth and Tenth streets, directly

across the avenue from Jefferson Market Courthouse. I had often noticed the place, but this was the first time I had ever been in it. Like most of the barrooms on Sixth Avenue in the Village, it was long and narrow and murky, a blind tunnel of a place, a burrow, a bat's cave, a bear's den. I learned later that many of the men and women who frequented it had been bohemians in the early days of the Village and had been renowned for their rollicking exploits and now were middle-aged or elderly and in advanced stages of alcoholism. I arrived at nine, which was when Gould and I had agreed to meet. He was nowhere in sight, and I went over and stood at the bar. "I'm just waiting for someone," I said to the bartender, who shrugged his shoulders. In a little while, I got tired of standing and sat on a bar stool. After I had been sitting there for half an hour or so, peering into the gloom, I recalled something that one of the first persons I had talked with about Gould had told me—a man who had been at Harvard with him. "If you're going to have any dealings with Joe Gould," he had said, "one thing you want to keep in mind is that he's about as undependable as it's possible to be. If he's supposed to be somewhere at a certain time, he's just as likely to arrive an hour or two early as an hour or two late, or he may arrive on the dot, or he may not show up at all, and in his mind Tuesday can very easily become Thursday." Around a quarter to ten, the telephone in a booth up near the front end of the bar began to ring. One of the customers stepped inside the booth and reappeared a few moments later and shouted out my name. When I stood up, startled, he said, "Joe Gould wants to speak to you."

"I'm sorry, but I won't be able to meet you tonight," Gould said, his voice sounding a little boozy. "I completely forgot that I had to go to a meeting of the Raven Poetry Circle. In fact, the meeting is going on right now, and I just slipped out and came down here to a phone booth in a drugstore to call you, and I have to go right back. I don't belong to the Ravens; they won't let me join—they blackball me every time my name comes up—but they let me attend their meetings, and now and then they give me a place on the program. The Ravens are the biggest poetry organization in the Village, and there isn't one real poet in the whole lot of them. The best parts of all of them put together wouldn't make one third-rate poet. They're all would-bes. Pseudos. Imitators of imitators. They're imitators of bad poets who themselves were imitators of bad poets. I can't stand them and they can't stand me, but the hell of it is, I enjoy them and I enjoy their meetings. They're so bad they're good. Also, after the program they serve wine. Also, there's a high percentage of unmarried lady poets among them, and sooner or later I'm going to bamboozle one of them into free love or matrimony, even if it has to be a certain tall, thin, knock-kneed drink of water I've had my eye on for some time now who's supposed to have a private income and writes poems about the eternal sea and has a Dutch bob and a long nose and an Adam's apple and always has cigarette ashes in her lap and cat hair all over her. 'Roll on, roll on,' she says, 'eternal sea,' and her big old Adam's apple bobs up and down. But the main reason I didn't want to miss tonight's meeting is I see a chance to poke some fun at the Ravens. Tonight is Religious Poetry Night, and I talked them into putting me on the program. I asked for a place right at the end. You can just imagine the kind of religious poetry they're capable of. Mystical! Soulful! Rapturous! 'Methinks' or 'albeit' in every other line, and deep—oh, my God, they're deeper than John Donne ever hoped to be. When they've all recited theirs, I'm going to stand up and recite mine. Listen, and I'll recite it for you. 'My Religion,' by Joe Gould:

> *In winter I'm a Buddhist,*
> *And in summer I'm a nudist."*

Gould giggled. He asked me if I had read the chapters of the Oral History he had given me. I said that I had, and that they had been a good deal different from what I had expected, and that I would like to read some more.

"The great bulk of the Oral History is stored away in a

place that's quite inaccessible," he said, suddenly becoming serious, "but I have a few chapters stuck away here and there around town where they're easy to get at. I'll tell you what. I have an old friend named Aaron Siskind, who's a kind of avant-garde documentary photographer, and he has his darkroom and his living quarters in a flat up over a second-hand bookstore at 102 Fourth Avenue, and I must have six, seven, eight, nine, ten, or a dozen composition books stuck away up there. He'll be in now—he works in his darkroom at night—and it's only a short walk from Goody's over to his place. Why don't you take a walk over there and read those chapters? He won't mind getting them out for you. And let's meet in Goody's tomorrow night. I promise you I'll be there this time."

Siskind's flat was over the Corner Book Shop, at Fourth Avenue and Eleventh Street, right in the middle of the second-hand-bookstore district. He came to the door, a short, jovial man with skeptical eyes, and I told him what I was after, and he laughed. "Good God!" he said. "Haven't you got anything better to do with your time than that?" However, he went at once to a clothes closet in the hallway of the flat and squatted down and looked around among the shoes and the fallen coat hangers on the floor of it and picked up five composition books. "Joe's a little off in his calculations," he said. "He has only five up here at present." He slapped the dust off the books and handed them to me, and I sat down and opened one. On the first page of it was carefully lettered, "DEATH OF DR. CLARKE STORER GOULD. A CHAPTER OF JOE GOULD'S ORAL HISTORY." This turned out to be another version of Gould's account of his father's final illness, death, funeral, and cremation. The facts in it having to do with these matters were the same as those in the version I had already read, although they were differently arranged, but the digressions were completely different. I opened the second book, and the title was exactly the same: "DEATH OF DR. CLARKE STORER GOULD, A CHAPTER OF JOE GOULD'S ORAL HISTORY." This was still another version. The title in the third book was "DRUNK AS A SKUNK, OR HOW I MEASURED THE HEADS OF FIFTEEN HUNDRED INDIANS IN ZERO WEATHER. A CHAPTER OF JOE GOULD'S ORAL HISTORY." This appeared to be an account of the trip that Gould had made to the Indian reservations in North Dakota. The title in the fourth book was "THE DREAD TOMATO HABIT, OR WATCH OUT! WATCH OUT! DOWN WITH DR. GALLUP! A CHAPTER OF JOE GOULD'S ORAL HISTORY." This was another version of the statistical chapter. The title in the fifth book was "DEATH OF MY MOTHER. A CHAPTER OF JOE GOULD'S ORAL HISTORY." This was the shortest of the chapters. It took up only eleven and a half pages, and most of it was a digression on the subject of cancer.

"Joe comes up here every few days and hits me for a

handout, or what he calls a contribution to the Joe Gould Fund, and if he happens to have a finished composition book with him he goes over and tosses it in the closet," Siskind told me as I looked through the books. "He's been doing that for quite a long time now. He leaves the books in the closet until anywhere from half a dozen to a dozen or so have accumulated, and then, one day, he gathers them up and puts them in his portfolio and takes them away. By and by, he starts a new accumulation. He used to ask me to read them, and I would, but I don't anymore. He writes on the same subjects over and over again, and I'm afraid I've lost interest in the death of his father and the death of his mother and the dread tomato habit and the Indians out in North Dakota and all that. He seems to be a perfectionist; he seems to be determined to keep on writing new versions of each of his subjects until he gets one that is absolutely right. One cold day last winter, he came up here and sat by the radiator and started correcting and revising one of his books. He went through it once, changing a word here and a word there and scratching out sentences and writing new ones in. Then he went through it again and changed some more words and scratched out some more sentences. Then he went through it again. Then he tore the whole thing up and threw it in the wastebasket. 'Jesus, Joe!' I said. 'You certainly improved that one. You improved it right out of existence.' "

"When he gathers up his composition books and puts them in his portfolio, where does he take them?" I asked.

"He's always been kind of vague and remote about that." Siskind said. "As a matter of fact, I've never really understood why he takes them away in the first place. I've often told him that he can leave them here as long as he likes, and that he can have the whole closet to himself if he wants it. He's such a perfectionist I wouldn't be surprised if he tears them up and throws them in the first trash basket he comes to. Then he starts all over again. Starts fresh. Oh, I guess he has some secret place or other where he takes them and stores them away."

THE NEXT NIGHT, I went into Goody's again. Gould was sitting at a table across from the bar. There was an empty beer glass in front of him. He was wearing the same dirty seersucker suit that he had been wearing at our first meeting, only now it was much dirtier and had a bad rip at the shoulder. It looked as if somewhere along the line someone had given his left sleeve an angry jerk, ripping it half off at the shoulder. I went over and sat down and returned the composition books and the little magazines that I had got from him, and thanked him for letting me read them.

"You were disappointed," he said accusingly.

"Oh, no," I said.

"Yes you were," he said. "I can tell."

"To be honest," I said, "I was. I understood from what you told me that the Oral History was mostly talk, but there wasn't any talk in the chapters you lent me or in the ones I saw at Siskind's."

Gould threw up his hands. "Naturally there wasn't," he said. "There are two kinds of chapters in the Oral History—essay chapters and oral chapters. As it happens, all those you read were essay chapters."

This remark instantly cleared up my puzzlement about the Oral History; it seemed to explain everything. I took Gould's empty glass over to the bar and got him a beer. Then, sitting down, I told him I would like very much to read some of the oral chapters.

"Oh, Lord," Gould said. "Since we've gone this far, there's something about the Oral History I'll have to tell you—something about its present whereabouts. I was hoping I could keep it quiet, but I can see now I would've had to let people know about it sooner or later anyhow." He frowned and cocked his eyes at the ceiling and stroked his bearded chin and seemed to be casting around in his mind for the simplest way to tell about something that was extraordinarily involved. "Oh, well, to go back a little," he said, "a woman I know who used to work in the main branch of the Public Library retired several years ago and bought a duck-and-chicken farm on Long Island, and last Thanksgiving she invited me out there. I'm not going to tell you her name or the exact location of her farm, so don't ask me any questions. It's an isolated place, out on a dirt road. Huntington is the nearest railroad station, but it's a considerable distance from Huntington. There are two houses on the place. One is a frame house, and a Polish farmer and his wife live in it and look after the ducks and chickens. The other is an old stone house, and my friend and a niece of hers live in it. My friend showed me over the house, including the cellar. The cellar was snug and dry and whitewashed, and it was partitioned into one large room and three small rooms. The small rooms were built to be used for storage, and had good strong doors. And the doors had locks on them—set-in locks, not padlocks. Now, early in January of this year, a month and a half or so after I was out there, a painter friend of mine told me that an art dealer had told him that the Metropolitan Museum was moving a good many of its most precious paintings to a bombproof location outside the city for the duration of the war, and I decided I'd better get busy and do something about the Oral History. I immediately thought of those rooms in my friend's cellar, and it seemed to me that one of them would be an ideal place for the Oral History. So I wrote to my friend and inquired into the possibility. She didn't think much of the idea at first—didn't want the responsibility—but I wrote to her again and said that a good librarian such as herself ought to be able to understand the importance to posterity of what I was asking her to do, and I promised her that generations yet unborn would be grateful to her and rise up and call her blessed, and finally she wrote and said for me to get the Oral History together and wrap it in two layers of oilcloth and tie some ropes around it—in other words, bale it up. I did so, and the following Sunday she and her niece drove in and picked it up and took it out and deposited it in her cellar. And that's where it is. And if you'll pay my train fare out to Huntington and back and my taxicab fare from the station out to her place and back and give me money enough to buy her a box of candy for a present, I'll take a run out there early next week and open the bale and select a couple of dozen representative chapters—oral ones, that is—and bring them in."

We figured out how much money he would need for the trip, and I gave it to him.

He took his time about making the trip. I didn't see him again until the following Thursday, when he came to my office and said that he had gone out to his friend's farm the day before but hadn't been able to get at the Oral History. "My friend wasn't home," he said. "According to her niece, she's been away a couple of months. She's down in Florida. She has a brother who's a retired high-school English teacher, a bachelor, and he was spending the winter in St. Augustine, and sometime around the middle of April he had a stroke. She's very attached to him, and she went down there to look after him. And just before she left, the niece said, she locked up half the place, including the three rooms in the cellar, and took the keys with her. This upset me, and I begged the niece to write her at once and ask her to send back the key to the room the Oral History is in. 'Write her yourself,' the niece said. 'It's none of my business.' Then I decided it might be a lot wiser to telephone her, so the niece gave me the number of the place where she's staying, and I'd appreciate it very much if you'd let me have money enough to make the call."

I said I could arrange for him to make the call right then, through the office switchboard.

"That would be fine," he said, "except I'm not supposed to call her during the day. The niece told me I should call her at night, because she's at the hospital during the day. If you'll just let me have the money, I'll call her tonight from the pay phone in Goody's."

Next morning, shortly after I got to the office, Gould telephoned and said that after calling the woman person-to-person several times he had reached her around midnight. "She must be all tired out and nervous," he said, "because she scolded me severely. She reminded me that when she agreed to store the Oral History she had made it clear that I couldn't be taking it out and putting it back in but that I'd have to let it stay put for the duration of the war. 'You wanted it in a safe place,' she said, 'and it's in a safe place, so just relax.' I asked her when she expected to return, but I didn't get much satisfaction out of her. 'It might be weeks,' she said, 'and it might be months, and it might be years. And in the meantime,' she said, 'quit bothering me.' I tried to reason with her, and she hung up on me."

"Would it do any good if I called her?" I asked.

"As soon as she found out what you were calling about," Gould said, "she'd hang up on you."

This put me in a predicament. Ever since my first interview with Gould, I had been tracking down friends and enemies of his and talking with them about him. Most of these people had known Gould for a long time and either were regular contributors to the Joe Gould Fund or had been in the past. In fact, several of them—E. E. Cummings, the poet; Slater Brown, the novelist; M. R. Werner, the biographer; Orrick Johns, the poet; Kenneth Fearing, the poet and novelist; Malcolm Cowley, the critic; Barney Gallant, the proprietor of Barney Gallant's, a Village night club; and Max Gordon, the proprietor of

the Village Vanguard, another Village night club—had
been giving him a dime or a quarter or a half dollar or a
dollar or a couple of dollars once or twice a week for over
twenty years. Each person I saw had suggested others to
see, and I had looked up around fifteen people and spoken on the telephone with around fifteen others. All of
them had been willing, or more than willing, to tell what
they knew about Gould, and I had got a great many anecdotes and a great deal of biographical information about
him from them. I had read the clippings concerning him
in the morgues of three newspapers. (The oldest clipping
I found was dated March 2, 1934, and was from the *Herald Tribune*. In it, Gould told the reporter that the Oral
History was 7,300,000 words long. In another clipping
from the *Herald Tribune*, dated April 10, 1937, he said
that the Oral History was now 8,800,000 words long. In
one from *PM*, dated August 24, 1941, Gould was called
"an author who has written a book taller than himself."
"The stack of manuscripts comprising the Oral History
has passed 7 feet," *PM* said. "Gould is 5 feet 4.") At the
suggestion of one of his classmates, I had gone to the library of the Harvard Club and hunted through the reports of his class—the class of 1911—for references to
him. I had spent a day in the genealogy room in the Public Library looking through New England genealogies and
town and county histories for information about his an-

cestors and family connections, and had been able to verify most of the statements he had made about them. Now all I needed was one more thing, a look at the oral part of the Oral History, but that seemed to me to be essential. As far as I was concerned, the Oral History was Gould's reason for being, and if I couldn't quote from it, or even describe it first hand, I didn't see how I could write a Profile of him. I could postpone further work on the Profile until the woman returned from Florida and let Gould into her cellar, but I knew from experience that postponing a project of this nature usually meant the end of it; I knew that my interest in it would fade as soon as I got involved in other matters, and that before long simply having it hanging over me would very likely cause me to turn against it. Furthermore, I was growing leery of Gould; I had begun to feel that, whatever the reason, he really didn't want me to see the oral part of the Oral History, and that when the woman returned, some brand-new difficulty might very well present itself. I decided on the spur of the moment that the best thing to do was to abandon the project right then and there and go on as quickly as possible to something else.

"I'm sorry, Mr. Gould," I said, "but I think we'd better just drop the whole thing."

"Oh, no!" Gould said. His voice sounded alarmed. "Look," he said. "I have an abnormal memory. In fact, people have often told me that I probably have what the psychologists call total recall. I've lost chapters of the Oral History several times and reconstructed them entirely from memory. Once, I lost one and reconstructed it and then found the one I had lost, and a good many pages in the two of them matched almost word for word. If you'll meet me in Goody's tonight, I'll recite some chapters for you. I'll recite dozens of chapters. If you've got the patience to listen, I'll recite hundreds. You'll get as good an idea of the oral part of the Oral History that way as you would by reading it. Considering my handwriting, you may even get a better idea."

That night, around eight, Gould and I sat down at a table in a quiet corner in the back of Goody's. First, he drank two double Martinis, doing so, he said, for a particular purpose. "I have found," he said, "that gin primes the pump of memory." Then he began telling the life story of a man he said he used to run into in flophouses who was a kind of religious fanatic and was called the Deacon, telling it in the first person, just as the Deacon had told it to him. The Deacon was a gloomy periodical drinker. He was a backslidden member of some schismatic Lutheran sect, he was under the impression that he had lost his soul, he believed that he had discovered hints in the Bible concerning the exact date—year, month, day, and time of day—of the end of the world, and he often saw things at night. One summer night, for example, while he was sitting in a doorway on Great Jones Street, near the Bowery, he smelled sulphur and looked up and saw the Devil walk past and felt the heat of Hell emanating from him. Later the same night, he saw two mermaids in the East River. They were off Pier 26, at the foot of Catharine Street, frolicking in the moonlight. "They weren't exactly half women, half fishes," he told Gould. "They were more like half women, half snakes. When they saw me sitting on the pier looking at them, they held out their arms and wriggled and made certain other motions trying to tempt me to come in with them, and if I had done so they would've wrapped themselves around me and dragged me to the bottom."

Gould spent an hour or so on the Deacon's visions and torments. Then, after drinking another double Martini, he quoted some remarks that he said had been made to him by a doleful old Hungarian woman, known as Old Budapest or Old Buda the Pest, who used to sit in bars on Third Avenue, around Cooper Square, and talk on and on to anyone who would listen. Gould said he had filled many composition books with her talk. Old Buda had been three times a wife and three times a widow; she had had some connection with the dope trade through one of her husbands; she had been a madam, or, as she defined it, "the operator of a furnished-room house for women over in the Navy Yard district in Brooklyn"; and she had wound up working in the kitchen of a city hospital. Her talk was made up for the most part of descriptions of and reflections on awful things that she had experienced or observed. Gould recited a few of her soliloquies verbatim and paraphrased others and summarized others. Finishing with Old Buda, he drank a fourth Martini—a regular one this time. Then he ordered another, but decided not to drink all of it. Instead, he ordered a large beer, drank it, and then ordered a small beer and drank it. At this point, he described an eating place in which he said he had spent a lot of time during the early thirties. It was called Frenchy's Coffee Pot; it was on First Avenue, near Twenty-ninth Street, just across from the Pathological Building of Bellevue Hospital, a building that also housed the City Mortuary; it stayed open until two in the morning and opened again at six; and it was patronized by nurses, internes, orderlies, ambulance drivers, morgue attendants, embalming-school students, and other people who worked in the hospital and the mortuary. Whenever he could, Gould said, he would engage these people in conversation, and now he began to quote some of the things they had told him. "This part of the Oral History is pretty gory," he said. "It is called 'Echoes from the Backstairs of Bellevue,' and it is divided into sections, under such headings as 'Spectacular Operations and Amputations,' 'Horrible Deaths,' 'Sadistic Doctors,' 'Alcoholic Doctors,' 'Drug-Addicted Doctors,' 'Women-Chasing Doctors,' 'Huge Tumors, Etc.,' and 'Strange Things Found During Autopsies.' "

Presently, after quoting at some length from each of his sections on Bellevue, Gould ordered another small beer and drank it, and then said that he would now quote for a little while from the longest and most important part of the Oral History. He said that he called this part "An Infinitude of Bushwa," and that it was about the Village, and that it ran through approximately seventy-five composition books. "It contains an enormous number of monologues, conversations, and disputes about a wide variety of art, literary, political, theological, and sexual matters that I overheard in the Village," he said, "and this will be very valuable to social historians in centuries to come, but the most valuable thing it contains is gossip—the things that people in the Village said about each other behind each other's backs during the twenties and thirties. As I say somewhere in my introduction to this part, which in itself takes up nine composition books, 'Malicious gossip, vicious and malicious. Spite and jealousy and middle-aged lust and middle-aged bile.' You can mention just about anybody who was around the Village during the last quarter of a century, and I've probably got something about him or her in this part of the History—something nasty. However and nevertheless and notwithstanding and be that as it may," he said, suddenly getting to his feet, "please excuse me a minute."

I had been so busy taking notes that I hadn't looked up for some time, and now I looked up and saw that Gould was drunk, or close to it. His eyes were blank and staring; he stared at me as if he had never seen me before. I was surprised, for his voice had been clear and his talk had been coherent. "I'll be right back," he said. Starting to step away from the table, he lurched into the aisle. Then, recovering himself, he made his way to the men's room, shuffling along cautiously and holding his arms out in front of him for balance, like a feeble old man.

When he returned, I said I was afraid that he was tired of talking, and suggested that we adjourn and meet again the following night. He shook his head vigorously. "I'm not in the least bit tired," he said. I closed my notebook and started to put it in my pocket. "You're the one who's tired," he said. He reached over and grabbed my sleeve. "Don't go yet," he said. "I want to say something about my mother. I didn't say much about her the other day in the diner, and I feel I should. Don't bother taking notes. Just listen."

His mother had been a good mother, he said, except for

one thing: She had never treated him as a grownup. While he was at Harvard, he said, and even after he had been living in New York City for years and had become well known as a bohemian and had grown a beard, she had occasionally sent him packages of a kind of penny candy, called peach pits, that he had liked as a child. This was typical of her, he said. "My mother did one thing to me when I was a boy," he said, "that I've never been able to forgive or forget. It may seem like a trivial incident to you, not worth thinking about twice, but I must've thought about it a thousand times. We were sitting in the parlor of our house in Norwood one evening after supper. I was studying, and I happened to look up and I saw that she was looking at me and apparently had been for some time and that tears were running down her cheeks. 'My poor son,' she said." Gould's eyes blazed. He was silent for a few moments. Then he forgot all about his mother and began talking about his father. He got wound up talking about his father; he couldn't seem to stop. His father had been a railroad enthusiast, he said, and a collector of timetables and of pictures of locomotives. Norwood is on a branch line of what was then the New England Railroad and is now the New York, New Haven & Hartford, and his father had been local surgeon for the railroad and a member of the International Association of Railway Surgeons. "One evening," Gould said, "my father put down his

newspaper, which was the Boston *Evening Transcript,*
you may be sure, and announced that he was going in to
Boston in the morning to see a new locomotive that the
railroad was getting ready to put into service, and then he
announced that he was taking me with him. This was
when I was around nine or ten, back before he had given
up on me, so to speak, and it was one of the happiest days
of my life. We got up before day and had breakfast together, and then we went in on an early train and stopped
in the station restaurant in Boston and had a second
breakfast. He had coffee and a cinnamon bun, and I had
hot chocolate and a cinnamon bun. Then we went out in
the yards. There was a crowd of railroad men standing
around the locomotive, looking it over, and my father
knew one of them. 'How do you do, Mr. Delehanty,' my
father said. 'This is my son Joseph.' "

Gould was so moved by this recollection that his voice
broke and his eyes filled with tears and he was unable to
continue talking. A few moments later, while he was dab-
bing at his eyes with a paper napkin and trying to regain
his composure, one of the old bohemians at the bar came
over to him and said, "I know how you feel, Joe. It was really quite a shock." Gould stared at the old bohemian.
"What shock?" he asked. The old bohemian stared back at
Gould. "Hearing about it," he said. "Hearing about
what?" asked Gould. "Bob," said the old bohemian. Then,

giving Gould a searching look and seeing that he was mystified, the old bohemian said that a man named Bob
Something-or-Other (I didn't catch his last name), who
was evidently another old bohemian and a friend of both
of them, had keeled over in Goody's during the afternoon,
while he was sitting at the bar, and had been taken to St.
Vincent's Hospital, where, according to a telephone call
the bartender had just received, he had died not long after
he arrived. Gould was visibly delighted by this piece of
news. "Well, I must say," he said, "I think that was very
commendable of Bob. In fact," he went on, "it's probably
the most commendable thing he ever did." The old bohemian was taken aback, but a moment later his face
changed and he laughed heartily. "Poor old Bob," said
Gould, in mitigation. Then he and the old bohemian became engrossed in an intensely serious discussion about
Bob's age—whether he had hit seventy or was still in his
sixties—and I took the opportunity to say good night and
depart.

Next night, Gould and I met again in Goody's. We met
at six, and I listened to him until around midnight. We
skipped the following night, which was Sunday night. On
Monday night, we met again at six, and once again I listened to him until around midnight. I thought that we had
agreed to meet at eight on Tuesday night, but when I arrived at eight I found that I had not made this clear to him

and he had been waiting for me since six and was so anx-
ious to start talking that he was in a state of agitation. To
square myself, I listened to him until Goody's closed, at
four o'clock in the morning. I saw him again on Wednesday night, and again on Thursday night, and again on Friday night. These sessions followed a pattern. Gould would
quote from the Oral History while the gin and beer were
gradually taking hold, and then he would lose interest in
the Oral History and talk more and more about himself,
until presently he would give up and talk about nothing
but himself. He seemed to think that no detail of his life
was too trivial to tell about. He would tell about the first
time he caught a fish or about the removal of his tonsils,
he would tell fatuous family anecdotes, laughing all the
while, and he would recall the ins and outs of conversations that he had had long ago with boyhood friends about
the mysteries of the adult world. Once, he pointed out
several scars on his cheeks and forehead and told how he
got each one; I remember that he got a couple of those on
his forehead when a Mason jar of stewed tomatoes that his
mother had put up exploded. Late one evening, he
paused for a moment and asked me if I was tired of listening to him, and I started to be polite and say "Oh, no!,"
but weariness made me frank and I said that I was, whereupon he snickered and said that he could sympathize with
me but that he had been waiting for years to talk to some-

one about himself and really go into detail, and now that he had an opportunity to do so he was going to make the most of it. "And since you're going to write about me," he said, "you can't help yourself—it's your duty to listen to me, it's part of your job."

After the Friday-night session, which lasted ten hours—it started at 6 P.M. and ended at 4 A.M.—I decided that I had become sufficiently familiar with a representative group of chapters of the Oral History and that enough was enough and that I wouldn't listen to him any longer, although it was obvious that he had scarcely got started and could go on for weeks; I simply didn't have the endurance. I tried to tell him this but found myself hesitating and dissembling, and he interrupted me. "If you're trying to tell me that you don't want to hear any more," he said, a little angrily, "you don't have to apologize. I'm perfectly well aware that I talk too much."

On the following Monday, which was June 29th, I started writing the Profile of Gould. On Tuesday, around noon, Gould telephoned and said he was worried about the facts concerning his family background that he had given me, and wanted to come up and interpret them for me. There were subtleties involved that I might miss, he said, since he was a New Englander and I was not. He came and stayed until deep in the afternoon, but he didn't interpret any facts; he simply talked some more about himself. On Wednesday, bright and early, he telephoned and said he had spent most of the previous night going over our talks in his mind, and had been shocked to discover that he had forgotten to tell me a great many very important things. He said he wanted to come up and give me this additional information. I told him that I was sinking and suffocating and drowning in information, and begged him not to tell me anything else until I had finished writing the first draft of the Profile and he had read it. He could point out the gaps in it then, I said. On Thursday, in the middle of the morning, the receptionist came in and said that he was outside and wanted to see me. "He says it's very important," she said. I asked her to tell him that I had gone to a funeral. He sat in the reception room for an hour or so, and then left a note for me with the receptionist and went away. "It is my recollection that I told you the title of the Greenwich Village part of the Oral History was 'An Infinitude of Bushwa,' " he wrote in the note. "After much thought, I have decided to change this title, and I felt that I should inform you of this decision at once. The new title is 'The Bughouse Without Bars, or Descents by Day and Descents by Night Into the Intellectual Underworld of Our Time.' If you have occasion to refer to this part of the O.H., please keep this in mind." On Friday, he telephoned, and I lied to him. I told him that I was going on vacation and would be away for two weeks. During these two weeks, I came to my office early and left late, I had no interruptions, and I finished writing the Profile. Then I did go on vacation.

Soon after I returned, early in August, Gould telephoned. By that time, the Profile had been put in proof, and I asked him to come up and read it. He read it slowly and carefully, and said he was pleased with it. "Is there anything in it you want me to change?" I asked. "Not a word," he said. Next day, he came in and said he thought that a paragraph having to do with his knowledge of sea gulls should be made much longer. "People are going to want to know a lot more about that matter," he said. Two days later, he came in with a similar suggestion about another paragraph. Three days after that, he came in with a similar suggestion about still another paragraph. He got in the habit of coming in at least once a week and trying to talk me into adding a few sentences here or a paragraph there. He never tried to get me to change anything; he just wanted me to put more in. On the majority of the days that he didn't come in, he telephoned me. The sound of his voice began to make me wince.

THE PROFILE OF GOULD was printed in the issue of *The New Yorker* for December 12, 1942, under the title of "Professor Sea Gull." The day before this issue went on the newsstands, I had to go down South, because of the sickness of a relative. I ran into some bad luck down there—I was thrown from a horse jumping a ditch and dislocated a shoulder, and while I was laid up from that I had pneumonia—and it was over three weeks before I returned to New York City; it was after the first of the year, in fact. When I got back to my office, there was a pile of letters on my desk from readers of the Profile. There were forty-five addressed to me, and seventeen addressed to Gould in care of me. Among the letters addressed to me was one from Gould himself.

"I have always had a feeling of being way ahead of my time," Gould wrote. "Consequently, I have always taken it for granted that the importance of the Oral History would not be recognized until sometime in the distant future, long after I am dead and gone, but now, thanks to your little piece, I am beginning to see signs that it may happen in my own lifetime. Strangers passing me on the street used to look at me with reactions ranging from bafflement to outright hostility, but now a steadily increasing number of them seem to know who I am and look at me with respect, and every now and then one of them stops me and ask questions about the Oral History. Serious and sensible questions. And people who really know me and have known me from old are beginning to look at me in a different light. I'm not just that nut Joe Gould but that nut Joe Gould who may wind up being considered one of the great historians of all time. As great as Froissart. As great as John Aubrey. As great as Gibbon. I have even noticed a change in the Village radicals. One of them who has been cutting me dead for a long time spoke to me the other day. He was patronizing, but he spoke. 'I know that you don't intend any such thing,' he said, 'but the Oral History may very well turn out to be a sort of X ray of the soul of the bourgeoisie.' 'What makes you think you know what I don't intend?' I asked him. It may also interest you to learn that the countermen and waitresses in the Jefferson Diner have begun to kid around with me again. When I go in there now, they call me the Professor or the Sea Gull or Professor Sea Gull or the Mongoose or Professor Mongoose or the Bellevue Boy, just as they used to, and I don't know why, but that pleases me. Sometimes, when they are kidding around, ignorant people like that have a kind of inspired audacity that is very cheerful and infectious. It lifts one's spirits. Book ignorant, that is. On some matters, I wish I knew one-tenth as much as they know. I still make the rounds of the places on Sixth Avenue, but I have a new hangout—the Minetta Tavern, at the corner of Macdougal Street and Minetta Lane, in the Italian part of the Village. The Minetta is an old-fashioned neighborhood bar-and-restaurant that attracts a few tourists now and then. The proprietor wants to encourage this, and he and I have reached what you might call an unspoken agreement. I sit at a table in there from late in the afternoon until around nine, ten, or eleven at night and work on the Oral History and give some Village atmosphere to the place. I am the resident bohemian, the house bohemian. In return, he sees to it that I get the table-d'hôte dinner free of charge so long as I order spaghetti and meat balls or something like that for the main course, and if I have to I can get by on one meal a day. Also, there are always people around who will buy me a beer or a glass of wine or if my need is great a Martini. Also, while talking to tourists and explaining the Oral History to them, I manage to pick up quite a few contributions to the Joe Gould Fund. . . ."

That night after work, I put the letters to Gould in my pocket and went down to the Minetta Tavern. Gould was sitting at the most conspicuous table in the place—it was up front and across from the bar and visible from the front window, on Minetta Lane—and he was busily writing in a composition book. I gave him the letters, and he looked at them with suspicion. Then, after reading a few, he got into a state of excitement and began ripping them open and glancing through them and murmuring appreciatively to himself. All the letters were complimentary in one way or another. One was from a woman in Norwood who had been in his class in high school. It was written in pencil on ruled paper, it was six or seven pages long, it contained news about a number of people Gould said he had not heard of since he'd left home, and it was very friendly. Gould's face shone as he read it. "Your old home is still one of the nicest-looking places in Norwood," the woman wrote. "People my age and older call it the old Dr. Gould house. It is now a rooming house for teachers and nurses and widows and women in general of the better class living alone. Do you recall Mrs. Annie Faulkner? She owns it and runs it. Her capacity is eighteen women. Inside it looks pretty much the same as when you lived there. Some of the furnishings are the same, such as that big tall mirror in the front hall with the gold cupids on it. If I remember right, you had some relatives living in Boston and other places in Massachusetts who were very well fixed, and sooner or later maybe one of them will leave you a little something and if this ever happens (and you know as well as I do such things do happen in widely related old families like yours full of old maiden aunts and cousins who might just as well leave it to you as to their dearly beloved old cats or dogs or the Christian Science Church the way they're always doing it) why don't you come on back up here and buy back the old house and live part of the year anyway in Norwood? I was very proud to read about the history book you are writing, and I heard others say the same, and someday I predict there will be a statue of you in Norwood. . . ." Several of the letter writers had enclosed dollar bills. "Buy yourself a drink on me," they wrote, or something to that effect. One, a Harvard classmate, had enclosed a five-dollar bill. Another, a retired Navy officer, had enclosed a check for twenty-five dollars. The retired Navy officer wrote that he spent a large part of his time sitting on the pier of a crab-picking plant near his home, in Annapolis, Maryland, watching sea gulls and listening to them. "I love sea gulls very much the way you do," he wrote, "and I sometimes feel that I, too, can understand their language."

I told Gould that I hoped he would write these people and thank them.

"Write them!" he said. "I'm going to get busy tonight and try my best to start a correspondence with each and every one of them. Maybe I can persuade some of them to become regular contributors to the Joe Gould Fund."

Gould went over to the bar to show one of the letters to a man he knew who was standing there. The composition book in which he had been writing was lying open on the table, and I looked at it. On the first page, in big, careful capital letters, was "DEATH OF DR. CLARKE STORER GOULD. A CHAPTER OF JOE GOULD'S ORAL HISTORY." I reflected that this was the fourth version of this chapter I had seen. When he returned, I said, "I see you're still working on the chapter about your father's death." This made him irritable. "Is there anything wrong in that?" he asked. "The other night, I got into a discussion about this very thing with Maxwell Bodenheim and some other old bohemians in Goody's. Max knows from perpetually looking over my shoulder that I've been working on my father's death for years. He knows I keep putting it aside and returning to it. And he was making fun of me for spending so much time on it. 'Don't tell me you're still trying to bury your father,' he said to me. Max himself has written a whole shelf of books—a whole shelf of novels, that is; a whole shelf of no-good novels; a whole shelf of *long* no-good novels—and he thinks that gives him the right to tell everybody else how to do. I told him that all I'm trying to do is write an account of the matter that will be a little masterpiece and last forever. That's all. 'Quality,' I told him, 'not quantity.' I told him that that little five-line poem I once wrote on the death of the *Dial* was worth more than all his claptrap novels put together. 'One five-line poem that's perfect of its kind,' I said, 'is worth more than any number of huge, formless, shapeless books.'"

The thought crossed my mind that this was an odd way for the author of a book as huge and formless and shapeless as the Oral History to be talking.

I had taken the letters to Gould on a Monday night. On the following Wednesday morning, another letter arrived for him. I forwarded it to him at the Minetta Tavern. On

Friday morning, four more letters arrived for him, and I decided to go by the Minetta that night on my way home and give them to him. Instead of which, shortly after lunch the receptionist stuck her head in my office and said that Gould was outside in the reception room and wanted to know if there was any mail for him. My heart sank. Oh, God, I remember thinking, I'm in for it now. He'll come in looking for letters practically every day from now on. And every time he comes in, he'll talk and talk and talk. And he'll keep on doing it, year in and year out, until I die or he dies. "Please send him in," I said. He came into my office, and I gave him the letters, and he looked each one over, front and back. "I wrote to all those people who wrote to me, just as I said I would," he said, "and these are the first replies."

"If you're going to keep on writing to them," I said, "wouldn't it be better to use the Minetta Tavern as your mail address?"

"If you don't mind," he said, his voice suddenly becoming indignant, "I'll continue to use *The New Yorker* as my address. The people at the Minetta are nice to me now, but they might get tired of me at any time and freeze me out, and if they did, I wouldn't like to have to go back there inquiring about my mail." Then he said something that brought me up short. "Look," he said. "You're the one who started all this. I didn't seek you out. You sought me out. You wanted to write a story about me, and you did, and you'll have to take the consequences."

"Please forgive me," I said. "You're right."

The next moment, Gould became conciliatory. "In other words," he said, giggling, "if you lie down with dogs, you have to expect to get up with fleas."

After that, just as I had feared, Gould started coming in frequently. He would come in two or three times a week, usually in the afternoon. When he was cold sober, Gould was shy—shy but desperate. He was a little like one of those men who are too shy to talk to strangers but not too shy to hold up a bank. If he was in this state when he came in, he would walk right past the receptionist and burst into my office without knocking and pick up his mail, if he had any, and collect a contribution to the Joe Gould Fund and snatch that morning's *Herald Tribune* out of my waste-basket and be out and gone in a matter of minutes. If he had been drinking when he came in, he would sit down and talk, and I would have to drop everything and listen to him. I didn't really mind this so much—in this state, he was apt to be full of whatever gossip was floating around at the moment in the barrooms and dumps of the Village, and I had developed a morbid interest in such gossip. Also, I could generally count on getting him out in half an hour or so. If he happened to be suffering from a hangover when he came in, however, my afternoon was shot. In this state, he was driven to talk, he was determined to talk, he would not be denied, and I would be lucky if I got him out in an hour and a half or two hours, or even three. He would sit on the edge of an old swivel chair in a corner of my office, his portfolio on his lap, his clothes smelling of the fumigants and disinfectants used in flophouses, rheumy-eyed, twitching, scratching, close to hysteria, and he would talk on and on and on. His subject was always the same—himself. And I would sit and listen to him and try my best to show some interest in what he was saying, and gradually my eyes would glaze over and my blood would turn to water and a kind of paralysis would set in. I was young then, and much more courteous to older people—and to everyone else, for that matter, as I look back on it—than I should have been. Also, I had not yet found out about time; I was still under the illusion that I had plenty of time—time for this, time for that, time for everything, time to waste.

I kept hoping that Gould would talk himself out, but the months went by and he showed no sign of doing so. He continued to come in as often as ever. One afternoon in August, during one of his visits, I suddenly realized, to my dismay, that as time passed, talking to me was becoming more and more important to him, instead of less and less. After a little reflection, I thought I saw why this was so. It didn't have much to do with me as a person. In fact, I don't think that Gould particularly liked me. He once said that he couldn't stand Southerners and that I was no exception, and although he was drunk when he said it, and apologized later, he probably meant it at least as much as he didn't mean it. It was simply that by listening to him for long sessions while I was working on the Profile and by continuing to listen to him whenever he came in and insisted on talking, I had probably come to know more about his past than anybody else in the city and perhaps than anybody else in the world, and had become a kind of stand-in relative of his, or fellow ex-Norwoodian. Despite the difference in our ages, when he talked to me he might have been talking to someone who had known him all his life. When he spoke of his Uncle Oscar, for example, he knew that I knew he was referring to his mother's brother, Oscar Vroom, whom his mother virtually worshipped, and he knew that I knew what his father thought of Oscar Vroom and what Oscar Vroom thought of his father. When he mentioned various people he had known while he was growing up in Norwood, such as Mrs. Betty Allsopp, he knew that I knew the parts they had played in his life. (He believed that Mrs. Allsopp was responsible for the fact that he had had a great deal of dental trouble and had had to start wearing false teeth before he was thirty.

Mrs. Allsopp was a family friend and lived across the street. She was a widow, she was his mother's age, and she was small and delicate and pretty. One hot summer day when he was around fourteen, she invited him into her kitchen for a glass of lemonade and he tried to pull up her dress and she slapped him so hard, according to him, that she deadened the nerves of eight of his teeth—four upper and four lower—and ruined his bite.) When he mentioned the Bigelow Block and the Folan Block and the Sanborn Block, he knew that I knew he was referring to store-and-office buildings that were landmarks in Norwood, and he knew that I was aware of some of the emotional connotations that their names had for him. When he spoke of Ed Goodbird or of Water Chief or of Ashkob-dip, he knew that I knew he was referring to old Indians he had known in North Dakota, and he knew that I knew how much he admired each of them, and why. In his years in the Village, he had pursued a succession of women bohemians, most of whom had been would-be poets or would-be painters, and many of whom had been alcoholics or extreme eccentrics, or both, and several of whom had wound up in state mental hospitals, and when their names came into his talk he knew that I knew which ones had been responsive to him and which ones had been unresponsive and which ones not only had been unresponsive but had complained about him to the police. He had given behind-their-back nicknames to many people in the Village, and when he referred to the Spitter or to the Nickel Snatcher or to Old Aunt Cousin Little Sister Susy Belle Susy Sue, he knew that I knew whom he meant. By knowing so much about his past, I had, in effect, I realized, become a part of his past. By talking to me, he could bring back his past, he could keep it alive. I realized also that there was no getting away from the fact that the more he talked to me the more I would know about his past, and the more I knew about his past the more important talking to me would become to him. This scared me, and I set out deliberately to get him off my back and, if necessary, onto somebody else's back as soon as possible.

The best way to do this, I decided, was to get an editor or a publisher interested in the Oral History. Gould had once told me that he had lugged armfuls of the Oral History into and out of fourteen publishing offices and had then given up trying to find a publisher for it. "Half of them said it was obscene and outrageous and to get it out of there as quick as I could," he said, "and the others said they couldn't read my handwriting." I had an idea that Maxwell Perkins, the editor at Scribner's who had worked with Thomas Wolfe, might possibly take an interest in

Gould, and I called him first. His secretary said he was out of town. I told her a little about Gould and asked her if she thought Mr. Perkins would see him and have a talk with him. "No," she said. "I don't." "Why?" I asked. "Mr. Gould has already been here," she said. "He came in out of the blue one day not long ago and insisted on seeing Mr. Perkins. I saw him instead, and he gave me two perfectly filthy copybooks to give to Mr. Perkins, each containing a manuscript chapter of his history. He seemed to think he might be able to get a large advance from Mr. Perkins on the strength of them. I spent most of the next day deciphering his handwriting and making copies of the chapters for Mr. Perkins to read. One chapter was about the death of his father, although it wandered all over the Western Hemisphere, and the other was something about Indians. Mr. Perkins read them and was not impressed. Some days later, Mr. Gould returned, and Mr. Perkins saw him and told him he was sorry but he couldn't give him an advance, whereupon Mr. Gould became quite difficult. I don't think Mr. Perkins would be at all eager to see him again."

A friend of mine named John Woodburn was an editor at Harcourt, Brace, and I called him next. Woodburn said that it had occurred to him several times that a representative selection of chapters from the Oral History might make a book, and that he would like very much to have a talk with Gould, but that he was too busy. He was working day and night going over a manuscript with a novelist who was leaving for Europe, he said, and he himself was supposed to leave on a business trip in a few days. Then, impulsively, he said that he would see Gould. "Ask him to come in at noon tomorrow," he said. "I have a luncheon date that I've been looking forward to, but I'll break it and have a sandwich sent in, and we can talk for at least half an hour. I have a number of questions I'd like to ask him about the Oral History, and you never can tell—maybe something will come of it." I telephoned Gould at the Minetta that night and told him about the appointment. He wanted to know if I knew anything about Harcourt, Brace's policy in regard to giving advances to authors against royalties and if so how much of an advance should he ask for, and he also wanted to know if I had ever seen a Harcourt, Brace contract and if so did it stipulate that the total amount of the advance would be paid upon the signing of the contract between author and publisher or did it stipulate that a certain percentage would be paid upon the signing of the contract and the rest upon the de-livery of the manuscript. I begged him not to talk to Woodburn about such things—it was entirely too early for that—but to spend the time describing the Oral History and answering Woodburn's questions. The next afternoon, Woodburn telephoned me. He was in a rage. Gould hadn't shown up. That night, I went down to the Minetta and saw Gould and asked him what had happened. He said he had gone into a bookstore and picked out some Harcourt, Brace books and looked them over and had come to the conclusion that Harcourt, Brace would not be the appropriate publishers for the Oral History and had decided not to keep the appointment. By the way he said "appropriate," he strongly implied that he did not think Harcourt, Brace was good enough to publish the Oral History. "Oh, for God's sake, Mr. Gould," I said. "Harcourt, Brace is one of the best publishing houses in the country, and you know it is."

I had another friend in the publishing business— Charles A. Pearce, of Duell, Sloan & Pearce—and a few days later I called him and discussed the matter with him. It turned out that he, also, had thought of the possibility of putting out a book of selections from the Oral History. "I'd like to have a talk with Gould and explore the idea," Pearce said, "but I don't want to make an appointment with him. If he broke an appointment with Woodburn, he'd most likely do the same with me. Also, I'd prefer to have a casual talk with him, so he won't start right away thinking about advances and royalty percentages and movie rights and North American serial rights and world-wide translation rights, and all that. Who does he think he is, anyway—Mary Roberts Rinehart? Suppose we do it this way. My office is only a few minutes from yours. The next time he comes in and sits down and it looks as if he's going to stay a while, why don't you call me, and I'll take a cab right up. I'll make it appear that I just happened to drop in." At that time, Pearce's firm was at 270 Madison Avenue, which is on the northwest corner of Madison Avenue and Thirty-ninth Street, and the distance from his office to mine was only four blocks up and one and a half over. On Friday afternoon, September 3, 1943, around three o'clock, Gould showed up in my office. He said that he had lost his fountain pen and that he wanted me to make a contribution to the Joe Gould Fund so he could buy a new one. He also needed some composition books, he said. Then he sat down in the swivel chair and began talking. He had a hangover, but it didn't seem to be a particularly bad one; that is, he was unduly talkative but he wasn't unduly incoherent. I excused myself and went into the next office and telephoned Pearce. Twenty minutes later, Pearce put his head in my door and said he had happened to be in the neighborhood and thought he'd drop in and say hello. "Please come in," I said, and I introduced him to Gould.

Pearce and Gould talked for a few minutes about a Village poet they both knew, and then Pearce said that he had been hearing about the Oral History for years and would like to read some of it.

" 'Some of it'!" said Gould. "Everybody wants to read 'some of it.' Nobody wants to just read it. From now on, I'm not going to let anybody read some of it. They'll read all of it or none of it."

"Well," Pearce said, "I'll do that. It may take me a long time, but if you'll bring it to my office or tell me where to go and get it, I'll make a start today or tomorrow."

"It's entirely too bulky," Gould said.

"Bring it in a little at a time," said Pearce. "When I finish reading one batch, I'll drop you a line and you can bring in another. I've often worked that way with authors of long books."

"It's stored in a place out on Long Island that's hard to get to," Gould said.

"We could hire a car over at Carey's limousine service, at Grand Central," Pearce said, "and drive out and get it. If you aren't too busy, we could drive out right now."

"I don't want to bring it back into New York City," Gould said. "I don't think it would be safe here. I don't think anything is safe here. I expect the whole place to go up in smoke any day now."

"We have some fireproof cabinets in the office that we keep manuscripts in," Pearce said, "and you could store it in one of them. We also have a big fireproof safe that we keep contracts in, and other important papers, and you could store it in there."

"What's the use?" said Gould. "After you got it, you probably couldn't read my handwriting."

"That's no problem," said Pearce. "We have a secretary in our office who's a wizard at reading hard-to-read handwriting. She prides herself on it. You could come in for a day or two and sit down beside her and help her until she got the hang of your handwriting, and then she could type up some chapters from various sections, and then, eventually, maybe we could publish a book of selections from the Oral History."

"No, indeed!" said Gould. "Absolutely not! It has to be published in its entirety. All or nothing."

"Well, now," said Pearce, "unless you let me read it—and you really don't seem to want me to—how can I tell if it's feasible to publish it in its entirety?"

Gould took a deep breath. "I've always been resolved in the back of my mind that the Oral History would be published posthumously," he said, "and I'm going to stick to that." He hesitated a moment. "There are revelations in it," he continued, "that I don't want the world to know until after I'm dead."

This stopped Pearce. He and Gould talked for a few

minutes about things unrelated to the Oral History, and then he said he had to be running along.

"If you ever change your mind," he said to Gould, "please give me a ring."

Gould gazed at him morosely and said nothing.

I was exasperated. As soon as Pearce was out of the room, I turned on Gould. "You told me you lugged armfuls of the Oral History into and out of fourteen publishing offices," I said. "Why in hell did you do that and go to all that trouble if you've always been resolved in the back of your mind that it would be published posthumously? I'm beginning to believe," I went on, "that the Oral History doesn't exist." This remark came from my unconscious, and I was barely aware of the meaning of what I was saying—I was simply getting rid of my anger—but the next moment, glancing at Gould's face, I knew as well as I knew anything that I had blundered upon the truth about the Oral History.

"My God!" I said. "It doesn't exist." I was appalled. "There isn't any such thing as the Oral History," I said. "It doesn't exist."

I stared at Gould, and Gould stared at me. His face was expressionless.

"The woman who owns the duck-and-chicken farm doesn't exist," I said. "And her brother who had the stroke doesn't exist. And her niece doesn't exist. And the Polish farmer and his wife who look after the ducks and chickens don't exist. And the ducks and chickens don't exist. And the cellar that the Oral History is stored in doesn't exist. And the Oral History doesn't exist."

Gould got up and went over to the window and stood there looking out, with his back to me.

"It exists in your mind, I guess," I said, recovering a little from my surprise, "but you've always been too lazy to write it down. All that really exists is those so-called essay chapters. That's all you've been doing all through the years—writing new versions of those chapters about the death of your father and the death of your mother and the dread tomato habit and the Indians out in North Dakota and maybe a dozen others or a couple of dozen others, and correcting them and revising them and tearing them up and starting all over again."

Gould turned and faced me and said something, but his voice was low and indistinct. If I heard him right—and I have often wondered if I did hear him right—he said, "It's not a question of laziness." Then, evidently deciding not to say any more, he turned his back on me again.

At that moment, one of the editors knocked on the door and came in with proofs of a story of mine. He said that some last-minute changes were having to be made in a story that had been scheduled to run in the next issue, and that because there might not be time enough to complete them, my story had been tentatively scheduled to run in its place, and that he would like to go over the proofs with me.

"Does it have to be done right now?" I asked.

"Well, as you might gather," he said, rather sharply, "we're kind of in a hurry."

I saw that I couldn't very well put this off, and I asked Gould if he would mind waiting in the reception room until I got through. He picked up his portfolio and went over and stood at the door. "No," he said, "I don't think I'll wait. I think I'll go on back downtown. The only reason I came up here today was to ask you for a contribution." I said that I would give him the contribution but that I wanted to ask him some questions about the Oral History first and that I hoped he would wait. He mumbled something and started down the hall toward the reception room.

The proofs took around half an hour. The second I got through with them, I went out to the reception room. Gould wasn't there. The receptionist said he had sat there for five minutes or so and had then left without saying a word. Well, anyway, I thought, I've got him off my back. God knows this wasn't the way I intended to do it, but I've probably got him off my back for good.

I returned to my office and sat down and propped my elbows on my desk and put my head in my hands. I have always deeply disliked seeing anyone shown up or found out or caught in a lie or caught red-handed doing anything, and now, with time to think things over, I began to feel ashamed of myself for the way I had lost my temper and pounced on Gould. My anger began to die down, and I began to feel depressed. I had been duped by Gould—I didn't think there was much doubt about that—and so had countless others through the years. He had led me up the garden path, just as he had led countless others up the garden path. However, I had thought about the matter only a short while before I came to the conclusion that he hadn't been talking about the Oral History all those years and making large statements about its length and its bulk and its importance to posterity and comparing it to such works as "The History of the Decline and Fall of the Roman Empire" only in order to dupe people like me but also in order to dupe himself. He must have found out long ago that he didn't have the genius or the talent, or maybe the self-confidence or the industry or the determination, to bring off a work as huge and grand as he had envisioned, and fallen back on writing those so-called essay chapters. Writing them and rewriting them. And, either because he was too lazy or because he was too much of a perfectionist, he hadn't been able to finish even them. Still, a large part of the time he very likely went around believing in some hazy, self-deceiving, self-protecting way that the Oral History did exist—oral chapters as well as essay chapters. The oral part of it might not exactly be down on paper, but he had it all in his head, and any day now he was going to start getting it down.

It was easy for me to see how this could be, for it reminded me of a novel that I had once intended to write. I was twenty-four years old at the time and had just come under the spell of Joyce's "Ulysses." My novel was to be "about" New York City. It was also to be about a day and a night in the life of a young reporter in New York City. He is a Southerner, and a good deal of the time he is homesick for the South. He thinks of himself as an exile from the South. He had once been a believer, a believing Baptist, and is now an unbeliever. Nevertheless, he is still inclined to see things in religious terms, and he often sees the city as a kind of Hell, a Gehenna. He is in love with a Scandinavian girl he has met in the city, and she is so different from the girls he had known in the South that she seems mysterious to him, just as the city seems mysterious; the girl and the city are all mixed up in his mind. It is his day off. He has breakfast in a restaurant in Fulton Fish Market, and then starts poking around the parts of the city that he knows best, gradually going uptown. As he wanders, he encounters and reencounters men and women who seem to him to represent various aspects of the city. He goes up Fulton Street and walks among the gravestones in St. Paul's churchyard, and then goes to certain streets on the lower East Side, and then to certain streets in the Village, and then to the theatrical district, and then to Harlem. Late at night, on Lenox Avenue, he joins a little group of men and women, some white and some Negro, who have just come out of a night club and are standing in a circle around an old Negro street preacher. He had seen the old man earlier, preaching at a street corner in the theatrical district, but had not listened to him. Now he listens. The old man is worldly wise and uses up-to-date New York City slang and catch phrases, but he also uses a good many old-fashioned Southern expressions, the kind that are mostly used by country people, and the young reporter realizes that the old man is also a Southerner, and, like himself, a country Southerner. His sermon is apocalyptic. There are fearful warnings and prophecies in it, and there are phrases snatched from bloody old Baptist hymns, and there are many references to Biblical beasts and fruits and flowers—to the wild goats of the rocks and to the pomegranates in the Song of Solomon and to the lilies of the field that toil not, neither do they spin. The old serpent is in it, and the Great Whore of Babylon, and the burning bush. Like the Baptist preachers the young reporter had listened to and struggled to understand in his childhood, the old man sees meanings behind meanings, or thinks he does, and tries his best to tell what things "stand for." "Pomegranates are about the size and shape of large oranges or small grapefruits, only their skins are red," he says, cupping his hands in the air and speaking with such exactitude that it is obvious he had had first-hand knowledge of pomegranates long ago in the South. "They're filled with fat little seeds, and those fat little seeds are filled with juice as red as blood. When they get ripe, they're so swollen with those juicy red seeds that they gap open and some of the seeds spill out. And now I'll tell you what pomegranates stand for. They stand for the resurrection. The resurrection of our Lord and Saviour Jesus Christ and your resurrection and my resurrection. Resurrection in particular and resurrection in general. All seeds stand for resurrection and all eggs stand for resurrection. The Easter egg stands for resurrection. So do the eggs in the English sparrow's nest up under the eaves in the 'L' station. So does the egg you have for breakfast. So does the caviar the rich people eat. So does shad roe." The young reporter intends to stay for only a few minutes, but he is held fast by the old man's rhetoric. Even though he feels that he has heard it all before a hundred times, he is enthralled by it. The old man reminds him of the Fundamentalist evangelists who were powerful in the South while he was growing up and who went from town to town holding revival meetings in big tents. He had hated and feared these evangelists—their reputations were based on the hideousness of their descriptions of Hell; the more hideous the description and the wilder the sermon, the better the evangelist was considered to be—but nevertheless they had left him with a lasting liking for the cryptic and the ambiguous and the incantatory and the disconnected and the extravagant and the oracular and the apocalyptic. He finds himself drawing oblique conclusions from the old man's statements in order to make them have some bearing on his own spiritual state. "All you have to do," the old man says, "is open your eyes and see the light, the blessed gospel light, and you can enter into a new time. You can enter into it and live in it and dwell in it and reside in it and have your being in it. You can live in the three times in one time. At one and the same time, believing in Him, you can live in the time gone by, you can live in the time to come, and you can live in the now, the here and now." As the young reporter listens, it dawns on him that it is not the South that he longs for but the past, the South's past and his own past, neither of which, in the way that he has been driven by homesickness to think of them, ever really existed, and that it is time for him to move out of the time gone by and into the here and now—it is time for him to grow up. When the sermon is over, he goes back downtown feeling that the old man has set him free, and that he is now a citizen of the city and a citizen of the world.

I had thought about this novel for over a year. Whenever I had nothing else to do, I would automatically start writing it in my mind. Sometimes, in the course of a subway ride, I would write three or four chapters. Almost every day, I would discard a few characters and invent a few new ones. But the truth is, I never actually wrote a word of it. Time passed, and I got caught up in other matters. Even so, for several years I frequently daydreamed about it, and in those daydreams I had finished writing it and it had been published and I could see it. I could see its title page. I could see its binding, which was green with gold lettering. Those recollections filled me with almost unbearable embarrassment, and I began to feel more and more sympathetic to Gould.

Suppose he *had* written the Oral History, I reflected; it probably wouldn't have been the great book he had gone up and down the highways and byways prophesying it would be at all—great books, even halfway great books, even good books, even halfway good books, being so exceedingly rare. It probably would have been, at best, only a curiosity. A few years after it came out, copies of it would have choked the "Curiosa" shelves in every secondhand bookstore in the country. Anyway, I decided, if there was anything the human race had a sufficiency of, a sufficiency and a surfeit, it was books. When I thought of the cataracts of books, the Niagaras of books, the rushing rivers of books, the oceans of books, the tons and truck-loads and trainloads of books that were pouring off the presses of the world at that moment, only a very few of which would be worth picking up and looking at, let alone reading, I began to feel that it was admirable that he *hadn't* written it. One less book to clutter up the world, one less book to take up space and catch dust and go un-read from bookstores to homes to second-hand book-stores and junk stores and thrift shops to still other homes to still other second-hand bookstores and junk stores and thrift shops to still other homes ad infinitum.

I suddenly felt a surge of genuine respect for Gould. He had declined to stay in Norwood and live out his life as Pee Wee Gould, the town fool. If he had to play the fool, he would do it on a larger stage, before a friendlier audi-ence. He had come to Greenwich Village and had found a mask for himself, and he had put it on and kept it on. The Eccentric Author of a Great, Mysterious, Unpub-lished Book—that was his mask. And, hiding behind it, he had created a character a good deal more complicated, it seemed to me, than most of the characters created by the novelists and playwrights of his time. I thought of the va-riety of ways he had seen himself through the years and of the variety of ways others had seen him. There was the way the principal of the school in Norwood had seen him—a disgusting little bastard. There was the way Ezra

Pound had seen him—a native hickory. There was the way the know-it-all Village radical had seen him—a reactionary parasite. There were a great many of these aspects, and I began to go over them in my mind. He was the catarrhal child, he was the son who knows that he has disappointed his father, he was the runt, the shrimp, the peanut, the half-pint, the tadpole, he was Joe Gould the poet, he was Joe Gould the historian, he was Joe Gould the wild Chippewa Indian dancer, he was Joe Gould the greatest authority in the world on the language of the sea gull, he was the banished man, he was the perfect example of the solitary nocturnal wanderer, he was the little rat, he was the one and only member of the Joe Gould Party, he was the house bohemian of the Minetta Tavern, he was the Professor, he was the Sea Gull, he was Professor Sea Gull, he was the Mongoose, he was Professor Mongoose, he was the Bellevue Boy.

I was still adding to the list when the receptionist cracked my door open and put her head in. "Mr. Gould has just come back," she said. "He was down at the lunch counter in the lobby all this time, having coffee."

"Bring him right in," I said. Then, for some reason—perhaps because of my new-found respect for Gould—I changed my mind. "No, don't," I said. "I'll go out myself and bring him in."

I stood up, and as I did so, a thought entered my mind

that caused me to sit back down. If I asked Gould the questions I had planned to ask him, I suddenly realized, and if he came right out and admitted that the Oral History did not exist—that it was indeed a mare's-nest—I might be put in the position of having to do something about it. I might very well be forced to unmask him. I found this thought painful. The Oral History was his life preserver, his only way of keeping afloat, and I didn't want to see him drown. I didn't want to blow the whistle on him. I didn't want to tear up his meal ticket, so to speak, or break his rice bowl. I didn't want to have to take any kind of stand on the matter at all. He wasn't harming anybody. He lived off his friends, it was true, but only off crumbs from their tables. Given a long life, he might yet write the Oral History. It would be better for me to leave things the way they were—up in the air. This was probably cowardly, but if it was, so it was. I was thankful now that when I pounced on him he hadn't admitted anything—he hadn't said yea, he hadn't said nay, he had said merely that it wasn't a question of laziness. And there was no law that said I had to ask him questions and try to trip him up and pin him down and worm the pure truth out of him. Suppose he chose to deny everything, and suppose he turned on me and denounced me, leaving it up to me to make the next move. I might be pretty close to certain of this, that, and the other, but I might have a hell of a

time proving it. While I was trying to make up my mind
what to do, Gould walked in, not bothering to knock.

"Are you going to give me the contribution?" he asked.

"Yes, I am," I said.

I gave him the money he wanted. He didn't thank me
but said what he usually said when someone gave him a
contribution to the Joe Gould Fund—"This will come in
handy." Then he went over and sat in the swivel chair and
put his portfolio on the floor at his feet. "You said you had
some questions you wanted to ask me," he said.

"I did have," I said, "but I don't now. There were some
things I thought I wanted to know, but I guess I really
don't. Let's just forget it."

A look of relief appeared on Gould's face. Then, to my
surprise, seeming to sense that I didn't intend to go one
bit further into the matter, he looked disappointed. I
could see from his expression that he wanted very much
to confide in me—it was that half-noble, half-fatuous expression that people put on when they have decided to
bare their souls—and once again my attitude toward him
changed. I became disgusted with him. I was doing my
best to keep from unmasking him, and here he was doing
his best to unmask himself. "Oh, for God's sake," I felt like
saying to him. "Don't lose your nerve now and start con-
fessing and confiding. If you've pretended this long, the
only decent thing you can do is to keep right on pretend-

ing as long as you live, no matter what happens." Instead, I said, "Please forgive me, but you really must excuse me now. It's getting late and I have some things I have to do."

This gave him the right to be huffy. "Oh," he said, "I'm ready to go. I've been ready to go for what seems like hours, but you held me up. After all, I've got things to do myself."

He picked up his portfolio and walked out without saying goodbye.

For quite a while after that, Gould distrusted me. He continued to come to see me, but nowhere near as often and never just to talk. He came only when he wanted a contribution to the Joe Gould Fund, and only, I suspect, when he was stony broke and couldn't run down any of his old reliables. He walked in and asked for what he wanted in as few words as possible and got it or some part of it and then stood around awkwardly for a few minutes and then hurried off. Although he continued to use *The New Yorker* as his mail address, he stopped asking for his letters the moment he came in, and, to preserve his dignity, waited for me to give them to him. Hoping to make things easier for him, I began forwarding letters to him at the Minetta. However, as an excuse to see how he was getting along, I would occasionally let a few accumulate and then go by the Minetta and give them to him. The

first few times I did this, I behaved as if nothing had happened, and sat down at his table as I always had, no matter whether he was alone or others were there, but I soon
found that if others were there my presence made him ill
at ease. If someone asked him something about the Oral
History, or even brought it into the conversation, he
would glance at me uneasily and try to change the subject.
I think he was afraid that at any moment I might stand up
and announce that there was no such thing as the Oral
History, that it was all imagination and lies. I made him
self-conscious; I got in his way; I cramped his style. From
then on, I never sat down with him unless he was alone. If
others sat down, I would look at my watch, and pretend to
be surprised at how late it was, and leave. Then, one
evening, Gould suddenly became his old self again. I was
sitting at his table when a couple of tourists, a man and his
wife, came over from the bar and asked him a question
about the Oral History. Without glancing at me and without any hesitation, he started describing the Oral History
for them, and in no time at all was comparing himself to
Gibbon—speaking of what he called "the fortunate im-
mediacy" of his position in relation to New York City as
contrasted with what he called "the unfortunate remote-
ness" of Gibbon's position in relation to the Roman Empire. I was greatly relieved to hear him talking like this,
not only because I could see that he had got over his dis-

trust of me but also because I could see that he had got his mask firmly back in place. Furthermore, I couldn't help admiring his spirit. He was like some down-on-his-luck but still buoyant old confidence man. He put his heart into his act. Right before my eyes, he changed from a bummy-looking little red-eyed wreck of a barfly into an illustrious historian. And the most he could hope to get out of the tourists was a few drinks and a dollar or two.

In the spring of the next year—the spring of 1944—a chance encounter that Gould had with an old acquaintance set some things in motion that made life easier for him for a while. Around eight o'clock one morning early in May, he left the Hotel Defender, at 300 Bowery, where he had spent the night, and started out on his daily round of soliciting contributions to the Joe Gould Fund. He was hungry, and he was suffering from a hangover, a bad case of conjunctivitis, and a bad cold. He intended to go first to the subway station at Sheridan Square and stand for an hour or so near the uptown entrance and waylay friends and acquaintances hurrying to work. On the way over, trying to pull himself together, he sat down on the steps of a tenement in one of the pushcart blocks on Bleecker Street. He threw his head back and started squirting some eye drops in his eyes, and at that moment a woman named Mrs. Sarah Ostrowsky Berman, who had come down to the pushcarts from her apartment on Union Square to buy some of the small, sweet Italian onions called *cipollini,* caught sight of him and impulsively went over and sat down beside him. Mrs. Berman was the wife of Levi Berman, the Yiddish poet, and she was a painter. She had come here from Russia when she was a girl, and while making a living sewing in sweatshops she had taught herself to paint. Although her paintings were awkward, they were imaginative and they had a hallucinatory quality, and they had been admired and highly praised by a number of people in the art world. She was a gentle, self-effacing woman, and somewhat other-worldly, and she was maternal but childless. She had often run into Gould at parties in the Village in the late twenties and early thirties and had had several long talks with him, but she had not seen him for years, and she was shocked by the changes that had taken place in him. She asked him how he was getting along on the Oral History, and he groaned and shook his head and indicated that he didn't have the strength right then to talk about the Oral History. She asked him about his health, and he pulled up his pants legs and showed her some sores that had recently appeared on his legs. Mrs. Berman got a cab and took him to her apartment. She made some breakfast for him. She washed his feet and legs and put some medicine on his sores. She gave him some clean socks and a pair of her husband's old shoes.

She gave him some money. Then, after he had gone, she sat down and made a list of all the people she knew who had known Gould in the period in which she had known him, including some who had moved to other parts of the country or to Europe, and she spent the rest of the day writing impassioned letters to them.

"Joe Gould is in bad shape," she wrote in one of these letters. "He is using up time and energy he should be devoting to the Oral History running around all over town getting together enough dimes and quarters for the bare necessities, and it is killing him. I have always felt that the city's unconscious may be trying to speak to us through Joe Gould. And that the people who have gone underground in the city may be trying to speak to us through him. And that the city's living dead may be trying to speak to us through him. People who never belonged anyplace from the beginning. People sitting in those terrible dark barrooms. Poor old men and women sitting on park benches, hurt and bitter and crazy—the ones who never got their share, the ones who were always left out, the ones who were never asked. Sitting there and dreaming of killing everybody that passes by, even the little children. But there is a great danger that Joe Gould may never finish the Oral History and that those anonymous voices may never speak to us. Something must be done about him at once. If it isn't, some morning soon he and a part of us will be found dead on the Bowery. . . ."

Among the people Mrs. Berman wrote to were two old friends of hers who had once been married to each other and had been divorced—Erika Feist and John Rothschild. Miss Feist was a German-born woman who had come here in the early twenties and had become a painter. Rothschild was a New Englander who had roomed with Malcolm Cowley for a while at Harvard and had got acquainted with Gould at a party in the Village soon after coming to New York City to make a living, and had been contributing to the Joe Gould Fund ever since. He was the director of a travel agency called The Open Road, Inc. One night a week or so later, Mrs. Berman received a long-distance call from Miss Feist, who, after her divorce, had moved from a studio in the Village to a farm in Bucks County, Pennsylvania. Miss Feist said that while she was married to Rothschild she had got to know and respect an old friend of his, a very reserved and very busy professional woman who was a member of a rich Middle Western family and had inherited a fortune and who sometimes anonymously helped needy artists and intellectuals, and that she had spoken to this woman about Gould. Independently of her, she said, Rothschild had also spoken to the woman about Gould. Miss Feist said that the woman had agreed to help Gould to the extent of sixty dollars a month. There were two conditions. First, Gould must never be told who the woman was or anything about her that might enable him to find out who she was. Second, some discreet and responsible person in New York City who knew Gould would have to receive the checks from the woman—they would come once a month—and disburse the money, passing it on to Gould in weekly installments and seeing to it that he spent it on room and board and not on liquor. It would have to be someone Gould respected and would heed. When Mrs. Berman heard this, she said, "Someone like Vivian Marquié," and Miss Feist said, "Yes, exactly." Mrs. Vivian Marquié was an old friend of Gould's and the proprietor of an art gallery on Fifty-seventh Street called the Marquié Gallery. As a young woman, she had been a social worker and had lived in the Village. She had met Gould at a party in 1925 or 1926 and had been helping him ever since. In recent years, she had been providing him with most of his clothes; she knew several men who were close to him in size, and she kept after them, and every now and then they gave her some of their old suits and shirts to give to him. He went to her gallery a couple of times a week for contributions to the Joe Gould Fund.

The following day, Miss Feist telephoned Mrs. Marquié at her gallery and explained the situation. Mrs. Marquié said that she herself had been worried about Gould and that she would be glad to handle the money and make it go as far as possible. Mrs. Marquié's maiden name was Ward, and she was a native of Lawrence, Long Island. Her husband, Elie-Paul Marquié, was a Frenchman. He was an engraver and etcher, and he was also a gourmet and an amateur chef. Through him she had become acquainted with a good many French people in the restaurant business. One of these was a man named Henri Gerard, who operated three rooming houses on West Thirty-third Street, between Eighth and Ninth avenues, just across the street from the General Post Office, that were known collectively as the Maison Gerard. They were old brownstones, and their numbers were 311, 313, and 317. In the basement of No. 311, he ran an unusually inexpensive restaurant that was also known as the Maison Gerard. Mrs. Marquié had a talk with Gerard about Gould. Gerard was used to the problems of people who had to get by on very little; most of his tenants were in that category. He said that for sixty dollars a month he could give Gould room and board and also see to it that he had a little left over for such things as cigarettes and carfare. His room would cost him three dollars a week, and he could get breakfasts for twenty-five cents, lunches for fifty cents, and dinners for fifty cents. Mrs. Marquié agreed to send Gerard a check at the end of each week covering

Gould's approximate expenses, and Gerard agreed to deduct what Gould owed from the check, and give him whatever was left over in cash. If he skipped a meal, he wouldn't be charged for it. If he skipped what seemed to be an undue number of meals, Gerard would let Mrs. Marquié know, in case he might be going without them in order to have some money to spend on liquor. Before the week was out, Gould was installed in a room on the fifth floor, which was the attic floor, of No. 313. In the days when the brownstone houses of this kind were private houses, all the rooms on this floor has been maids' rooms, and Gould's room had obviously been the one that was customarily occupied by the newest, greenest maid. It was around behind the banisters at the top of the stairwell, it had a skylight instead of a window, and it was just big enough for a bed, a chair, a table, and a dresser.

At first, Gould wasn't able to get much pleasure out of living at the Maison Gerard or out of anything else connected with his new way of life, for the mystery of the identity of his patron tormented him. It was all he could think about. For a while, he turned up at Mrs. Marquié's gallery at least once a day, and sometimes as often as three or four times a day, and asked her seemingly innocent questions in an effort to trick her into giving him some clue. She begged him to stop it, but he couldn't. The speculation that seemed most likely to him was that it was someone who had been in his class at Harvard, and Mrs. Marquié encouraged him to believe this. Then, one day, instead of using the phrase "your patron," she forgot herself and used the word "she," and that inflamed Gould's imagination. He spent every afternoon for a couple of weeks going through newspaper files in the Public Library and searching for information about rich women in general and rich women who were patrons of the arts in particular, but he wasn't able to find any clues. His mind was dominated for several days by the idea that the woman might somehow be one or the other of two well-to-do old spinster sisters who were cousins of his and lived together in Boston. He had always been afraid of them, and he hadn't seen or heard of them since a few years after he got out of Harvard, when he had asked them to lend him some money with which to revisit the Indian reservations in North Dakota and they had refused. However, he finally got up his nerve and called them collect. One of them accepted the call and listened to him for about a minute while he tried in a roundabout way to find out what he wanted to know, and then interrupted him and said that she couldn't imagine what he was leading up to but that, whatever it was, she didn't want to hear it and that if he ever called her or her sister again she would put the police on him. Two or three nights later, lying in bed unable to sleep, he recalled an elderly woman, reputed to be very rich, whom he had once met at a party on Washington Square and with whom he had had a pleasant conversation about Edgar Allan Poe, and he decided that *she* might be the woman. In the morning, after a chain of telephone calls, he found out that she was dead. Next, he got it in his head that it might be some woman who had become interested in him through reading the Profile and that I knew who she was, and he came to me and asked me for her name. He demanded her name. Years later, quite by chance, I did find out who the woman was, and went to see her and had a talk with her, but at that time I didn't know who she was, and I told Gould so. He went away unconvinced and returned a few days later with a long letter that he had written to the woman. He wanted me to read it and send it on to her. The letter had a preamble, all in capitals, which read, "A RESPECTFUL COMMUNICATION FROM JOE GOULD TO HIS UNKNOWN PATRON (WHO WILL BE CHERISHED BY POSTERITY FOR HER GENEROSITY TO THE AUTHOR OF THE ORAL HISTORY WHETHER SHE CHOOSES TO REMAIN ANONYMOUS OR NOT) PROPOSING THAT INSTEAD OF 60 DOLLARS MONTHLY SHE GIVE HIM A LUMP SUM OF 720 DOLLARS YEARLY THE PRINCIPAL ARGUMENT BEING THAT THIS WOULD PERMIT HIM TO GO ABROAD AND LIVE IN FRANCE OR ITALY WHERE BY EXERCISING A LITTLE PRUDENCE WHICH HE IS FULLY PREPARED TO DO THE MONEY WOULD GO TWICE AS FAR." It seemed to me that Gould's purpose in writing this letter was to provoke the woman into some kind of communication with him, no matter what, and this alarmed me. I urged him to tear the letter up and forget about lump sums and living abroad, and all the rest of it, or the woman might hear that he was already complaining and get annoyed and cut the money off. If he went ahead and finished the Oral History, or at least got some work done on it, I said, maybe she would come forth and make herself known to him. He told me to stop giving him advice; he could handle his own affairs. Then, a moment later, an agonized look appeared on his face and he exclaimed, "I'd almost rather know who she is than have the money!" He stopped talking until he had got control of himself. "How would you feel," he went on presently, "if you knew that somewhere out in the world there was a woman who cared enough about you not to want you to starve to death but at the same time for some reason of her own didn't want to have anything to do with you and didn't even want you to know who she was?" He watched me craftily. "A woman who had an illegitimate baby when she was young and hated the father of it and let it be adopted might behave that way," he said, "if she got to be old and rich and respectable and suddenly found out by reading a Profile in *The New Yorker* that the baby was now a middle-aged man living in poverty on the Bowery." He paused for a moment. "I know I sound crazy," he continued, "but when I was a boy I used to daydream that I had been adopted, and lately I've been having those daydreams all over again." He left the letter on my desk and went away, and a few days later he returned and retrieved it and took it up to Mrs. Marquié and asked her to read it and send it on to the woman. Mrs. Marquié had always been gentle with Gould, but at this point she spoke sharply to him, and something she said must have brought him to his senses, for from that time on he kept his curiosity about his patron to himself.

Not long after this, Gould stopped coming to my office (I had begun forwarding letters to him at the Maison Gerard), and I lost track of him for a while. I saw him around the middle of June. During the next six months, for one reason or another, I spent more time out of New York City than in it, and I didn't see him again until one afternoon in December. On that afternoon, I was walking past the Jefferson Diner when I heard the peremptory sound of metal rapping on glass, and looked up and saw Gould staring out at me from a booth in the diner and rapping on the window with a coin to get my attention. I went in and sat down with him. "Hold on to yourself and don't faint," he said, "and I'll buy you a cup of coffee."

It was the same booth we had sat in when I had my first talk with him. His face and hands were as dirty as ever, but his color was good and his eyes were clear and he had put on a little weight. As usual, he had on a suit that was a size or two too big for him. It was somebody's castoff—the ruins of a suit—but it was well cut and it was made of some kind of expensive, Scottish-looking material, and it had been a good suit in its time. He even had on the vest. He wore a hat whose sides were deeply dented and whose brim was turned up on one side and down on the other. It was an extraordinarily rakish hat, and almost any veteran Villager could have identified it at a glance; it was one of E. E. Cummings's old hats. I told Gould that he looked the best I had ever seen him, and I was surprised at the smugness of his response.

"Oh, I'm doing all right," he said, smiling complacently. "I'm doing fine. I didn't much care for the Maison Gerard at first, or the Maison G., as the inmates call it—it's too out-of-the-way, the food is too starchy, and the stairs are a damned nuisance—but I've gotten used to it. In fact, I'm quite happy there. I come down to the Village and make the rounds the same as ever and scratch around for contributions to the Joe Gould Fund, but it isn't a life-and-death matter any longer. I've even stopped bothering with some people—the dime ones and the maybe-tomorrow ones. I just hit the ones I'm sure of, and I don't hit them as often as I used to. A peculiar thing has happened. I thought I'd be ruined in the Village if the news got out that I had a patron who was paying for my room and board, and I tried to keep it under my hat, but I couldn't; I told a few of my friends and they told others, and one by one all of them found it out, and what do you know—instead of reducing the amount of their contributions or refusing to give me anything at all anymore, they've become far more generous than they used to be. People who used to give me a quarter and give it grudgingly now give me fifty cents, and sometimes even a dollar, and give it willingly. You know the old fundamental rule: 'Them as has gits.' Sometimes, these days, I have three, four, five, six, seven dollars in my pocket. I don't bum cigarettes any longer, let alone smoke picked-up butts; I buy my own. Sometimes I even drop in a place and order a drink and pay for it myself. And I'm taking better care of myself. Most mornings, if I don't have a hangover, I get up around eleven and have a big breakfast, and then I walk up to the main branch of the Public Library and read the papers or look up something, or I might go to a few exhibitions in the galleries on Fifty-seventh Street and see if there are any good nudes, or I might take a run up to the Metropolitan or the Frick or the Museum of Natural History or the Museum of the American Indian, or I might just walk around the streets. After a while, I go back to the Maison G. and lie down for an hour or so, and then I have an early dinner, and then I get on the subway and go down to the Village. I knock around the Village until the bars close at

4 A.M. and everybody goes home, and then I head on back to the Maison G. Compared to the way things used to be, I'm living the life of a millionaire." He hummed the tune of a bitter old Bessie Smith song and then sang a few words. " 'Once I lived the life of a millionaire,' " he sang in his squeaky, old-Yankee voice. " 'Spending my money, I didn't care. . . .'

"Of course," he went on, "there's one thing I *do* keep under my hat, and that's the fact that I don't know who my patron is. I don't give a damn anymore who she is, but I have my pride. People keep asking me, and I tell them I'm not allowed to say. It's a famous name, I tell them, and they'd recognize it if I mentioned it—one of the richest women in the world. I call her Madame X, and I hint that I have the inside track with her. You know how bohemians are. They profess to disdain money, but they lose all control of themselves and go absolutely berserk at the slightest indication of the remotest hint of the faintest trace of a smell of it. Ever since the word got out that I have a patron, and not only that, a *woman* patron, and not only that, a *rich* woman patron, the poets and the painters have been getting me aside and buying me drinks and asking me to tell Madame X about their work. I try to be as helpful as I can. 'Let me have a few of your best poems,' I say if it's a poet, or 'Let me have a few of your best sketches,' I say if it's a painter, 'and I'll take them up and show them to Madame X the next time I go up to see her in her huge town house just off Park Avenue.' I take the poems or the sketches up to my room at the Maison G. and put them on the dresser and leave them there for a week or two, and then I take them back to the genius who produced them. 'Madame X looked at your work,' I tell him, 'and she asked me to thank you very much for letting her look at it.' 'But what did she say about it?' the genius asks. 'She strictly forbade me to tell you,' I say, 'but we've been friends for a long time, and I know you too well and respect you too much to lie to you, and I'm going to tell you exactly what she said. She said that she couldn't detect the slightest sign of any talent whatsoever in your work, and she said she feels it would be very wrong of her to encourage you in any way.' "

Gould's eyes flashed, and he giggled. "Oh," he said, "I've put quite a few people in their places that way. I've settled quite a few old scores that way."

I found myself getting annoyed with Gould, not because of his gloating over the settling of old scores—that was all right with me; I believe in revenge—but because of his general air of self-satisfaction, and I asked him a malicious question. "How are you getting along on the Oral History?" I asked.

"Fine!" he said, not batting an eye. "I'm making a lot of progress on it." His portfolio was beside him in the booth, and he patted it. "I've added an enormous number of words to it lately," he said. "It's growing by leaps and bounds."

As time went on, Gould grew accustomed to having his room and board paid for by his unknown patron. He came to take it for granted and to look upon it as a permanent arrangement. One morning in November, 1947, after he had been living at the Maison Gerard for almost three and a half years, I had a telephone call from him, and the moment I heard his voice I knew that something was wrong. "Mrs. Marquié called me yesterday afternoon and asked me to come up to her gallery at once," he said. "I went up there, and she broke the news to me that some weeks ago she had received word that Madame X was thinking of stopping her subsidy to me but that a man and a woman she knows who are old friends of Madame X were trying to persuade her to keep it going. She hadn't wanted to tell me anything about it, she said, until she had found out for certain just what Madame X was going to do. Well, she found out for certain yesterday. Madame X sent word to her that she was putting a check for December in the mail but that that would be the last." Gould paused for a moment and I heard him take a deep breath. "I asked Mrs. Marquié to tell me why Madame X had turned against me," he said. "I begged her to tell me. She said she simply didn't know." He paused again. "Not knowing who she is was bad enough," he said, "but not knowing why she's turned against me is nerve-racking." He paused once again. "It's the worst news I've ever had in my life," he said. "I haven't been able to keep anything on my stomach since I heard it."

Gould sounded hurt and bewildered and terribly forsaken, and he also sounded humiliated. There was something in his voice, a hint of panic, that stayed in my mind and made me uneasy. In the middle of the afternoon, I left the office and took a taxicab to the Maison Gerard. A porter vacuum-cleaning the carpet in the vestibule said that Gould had gone out but that he might have come back in. "Go on up and see," he said. "His room'll be open. He never locks it." Gould wasn't in. Standing in the door and peering into his room, I saw some composition books on his dresser, and I went over and looked at them. There were five of them. I took the liberty of opening the one on top. On the first page was the old familiar title: "DEATH OF DR. CLARKE STORER GOULD. A CHAPTER OF JOE GOULD'S ORAL HISTORY." I went ahead and opened the second one. The title read, "THE DREAD TOMATO HABIT. A CHAPTER OF JOE GOULD'S ORAL HISTORY." I opened the third one. The title read, "DEATH OF DR. CLARKE STORER GOULD. A CHAPTER OF JOE GOULD'S ORAL HISTORY." I opened the fourth one. The title read, "DEATH OF DR. CLARKE STORER

GOULD. A CHAPTER OF JOE GOULD'S ORAL HISTORY." I opened the fifth one. The title read, "DEATH OF DR. CLARKE STORER GOULD. A CHAPTER OF JOE GOULD'S ORAL HISTORY." I put the books back the way they were and left the room. "God pity him," I said, "and pity us all."

When Gould's subsidy ran out at the end of December, he told Gerard that he wanted to keep on staying at the Maison Gerard. He would give up the board part of his room-and-board arrangement, at least for a while, he said, and concentrate on trying to hold on to his room. It was obvious that he hoped to do this by redoubling his efforts in soliciting contributions to the Joe Gould Fund. However, he forgot the old fundamental rule that he had once referred to—"Them as has gits"—and made the mistake of telling his friends that he had lost his patron. Consequently, a good many of them, fearing that he would now become too dependent on them, began cutting down on their contributions. Before long, it became hard for him to get together three dollars in a lump sum for his weekly rent, and Gerard refused to let him pay by the night. "You are penalizing me because I don't live the way most people do," Gould told him. "Most people live on a week-to-week basis or on a month-to-month basis. I live on a day-to-day basis, and some days I live on an hour-to-hour basis." "I know all that, and I would like to help you," Gerard replied, "but the Maison Gerard is not a flophouse."

By the end of February, Gould was in debt to Gerard. He had set fire to his bed at the Maison Gerard several times by falling asleep while smoking. In March, he set fire to it again, and, using this as an excuse, Gerard asked him to leave. At that time, there was a cluster of cheap hotels around Tenth Avenue and Forty-second Street. In one of them, the Watson Hotel, at 583 Tenth Avenue, it was possible to get a room—that is, a narrow cubicle furnished with a metal cot—for thirty-five cents a night, and Gould began staying there. Late one night, leaving a barroom in the lower Village and feeling too tired to take the subway and go uptown to the Watson, he walked over to the Bowery and got a bed in a flophouse, and found himself right back where he had started from in May, 1944. Next day, he decided that he might as well keep on staying in Bowery flophouses, since the Bowery was so convenient to the Village, and from that time on almost every step he took was a step going down.

It soon became apparent to people who had known Gould through the years that a change had taken place in him. "What's the matter with you, Joe?" I heard one of the old bohemians in Goody's say to him one night. "You don't seem to be yourself." "I'm *not* myself," he answered. "I've never been myself." He made the rounds in the Village as he always had, turning up during the afternoon and night in at least a dozen barrooms, cafeterias, diners, and dumps, but he began to look as if he didn't belong in these places. More often than not, he was abstracted or gloomy or withdrawn or had a faraway look in his eyes. One night, I went into a place in the Village called Chumley's for dinner. As I sat down in the dining room, I glanced through an archway at the bar, which was in an adjoining room, and there was a crowd of loud, laughing, joking, overstimulated men and women sitting or standing two deep along it, and down at the end of it I saw Gould's somber, bearded face. He was standing by himself, holding a beer, observing the others, and he had on a ragged suit and an old dog's bed of an overcoat, and he was all hunched up, and he looked remarkably separate and set off from everybody else. He looked like the ghost of Joe Gould come back to haunt the bar in Chumley's. He looked like a zombie.

He continued to go to the Minetta every night and sit for a few hours at his customary table and scribble in a composition book in full view of any tourists who might happen to be around, but when tourists came over and asked him what he was working on he rarely made big, bragging speeches any longer. His replies were more likely to be sarcastic or scurrilous or wearily offhand. Not that the tourists minded; they seemed to think that that was exactly the way a bohemian should behave, and they showed just as much interest in the Oral History and contributed just as much to the Joe Gould Fund as the ones he used to knock himself out trying to impress.

It began to take him longer and longer to get over the effects of drinking, and his drinking habits changed. While he was living at the Maison Gerard, he had got used to holing up in his room all day if he had a hangover and sleeping it off, but he couldn't do that in flophouses, and he developed a dread of hangovers. Instead of drinking anything and everything every chance he got—the stronger the better, the hell with tomorrow—as he had been doing, he began sticking to beer. No matter how hard a party of tourists might try to persuade him to order something stronger, he would insist on beer. Even so, by spacing the beers out, he managed to stay in a fairly constant state of mild intoxication. In this state, he was easily irritated, and his speech became looser all the time. He began to make spiteful or uncomfortably frank remarks to old friends, and he began to tell people whom he had always pretended to like what he really thought of them. Once, staring across a cafeteria table at a man he had known ever since they were young men in the Village together, he said, "*You* certainly sold out." "You're slipping," he once told Maxwell Bodenheim. "You were a better poet twenty-five years ago than you are now, and you weren't any good then." On another occasion, he told

Bodenheim that he wasn't a real poet anyhow. "You're only an artsy-craftsy poet," he said. "A niminy-piminy poet. An itsy-bitsy poet. And you're frightfully uneducated. You don't know how to punctuate a sentence, and all you've ever read is Floyd Dell and Ethel M. Dell and the Rubáiyát."

In those years, I used to go downtown at night on the Fifth Avenue bus. I usually got off at my stop, at Tenth Street, around seven-thirty. Gould knew this, and about once a week he would be waiting for me. When I stepped off the bus, he would appear out of the shadows in the doorway of the Church of the Ascension, on the corner, and hurry over to the bus stop and join me. He would walk a little way up the street with me and I would give him a contribution, and then he would dart off into the night. Sometimes we would stand on the street and talk for a few minutes. One night in the summer of 1952, as we were standing talking, he told me rather hesitantly that he was worried about his health. He had been having dizzy spells, he said. "The other day," he said, "I got on the subway at Fourteenth Street, intending to get off at the Twenty-third Street station, and a moment after I sat down, I had a kind of blackout, and when I came to, the train was pulling into the station at Seventy-second Street." I told him that a doctor I knew had read the Profile of him with great interest, and often asked me questions about him and about the progress he was making on the Oral History. "He said one time that if you ever needed medical attention he'd be glad to see you and wouldn't charge you anything," I told Gould. I asked him to let me call the doctor and make an appointment for him. Gould shook his head. "Ah," he said, looking vaguely up the street, "what's the use?"

Around the middle of December of that year, I became conscious of the fact that I hadn't seen Gould at the bus stop for several weeks, but I didn't think much about it. It wasn't at all unusual for Gould to disappear from the Village for a few days or a few weeks, or even a few months, and then suddenly reappear and give an odd explanation for his absence. "I went on a bird walk along the waterfront with an old countess," he once said after such an absence. "The countess and I spent three weeks studying sea gulls." Another time, after he had been away unaccountably for most of a summer, he told people that he had been on a cruise on a yacht. "J. P. Morgan's yacht," he said.

In January, 1953, I went to a party at the house of a psychiatrist I had known ever since I was a young reporter and covered Bellevue Hospital and the Medical Examiner's office. Among the other guests was a woman psychiatrist who was on the staff of Pilgrim State Hospital, which is out in Suffolk County, Long Island, at a place called West Brentwood. I had seen her several times before at my friend's house and had always enjoyed talking with her, not about psychiatry—we never talked about that—but about things like the feeding habits of striped bass; she was an obsessed surf caster. This evening, when I spoke to her, she told me that she was taking a leave of absence from the hospital to have a baby. Then she said she had something she wanted to tell me, and we walked over and stood by a window. "We have an old friend of yours out at Pilgrim State," she said. "The man you wrote about who's the author of 'An Oral History of the World,' or whatever it is he calls it. Joe Gould." She said that Gould had collapsed on the Bowery one afternoon around the middle of November and that an ambulance from Columbus Hospital had picked him up. He was found to be suffering from "confusion and disorientation," and Columbus, which doesn't have a psychiatric service, had transferred him to the psychiatric division at Bellevue. Bellevue had kept him under observation until sometime around Thanksgiving, and had then transferred him to Pilgrim State.

"What's the matter with him?" I asked. "What do you call it?"

"It's nothing at all strange or unusual," she said. "Arteriosclerotic senility. The same thing a lot of us will have if we live long enough. Only, in his case it hit him rather early—he's only sixty-three. Also, he has something wrong with his kidneys. Also, since he's been out at Pilgrim State he's had a staggering number of minor ailments, one right after another. That often happens to men of his type, the Bowery type, once they finally get into a hospital. Among other things, he's had the worst case of conjunctivitis I've ever seen, an acute attack of bursitis, a terrible boil on the back of his neck, a series of chills, a series of earaches, and a persistent pain of some kind in his stomach. And I suspect he's just getting started."

I asked about visiting him.

"I wouldn't, if I were you," she said. "Right now, he's so suspicious and confused it might do him more harm than good. He probably wouldn't know you. And if he did, trying to talk to you would just tire him out. As a matter of fact, if you want to do him a great favor, don't tell his friends in the Village where he is. At least, not now. Just keep it to yourself. Just forget I ever told you. We had another well-known bohemian in Pilgrim State a year or so ago, and people from the Village came out in droves to visit him, men bohemians and women bohemians, big bohemians and little bohemians, old bohemians and young bohemians, their tongues going a mile a minute, and they certainly didn't do him any good. Every time we got him to the point where he seemed to be almost reaching shore, so to speak, some of them would come out and push him back in. They'd push him back in and hold his head under. The main reason they came out wasn't to see him anyway but to try and get one of the psychiatrists aside and impress him or her with how much they knew about psychiatry—a subject, I might add, about which they were fantastically ill-informed."

I decided that for the time being I would do as she said and keep Gould's whereabouts to myself.

Pretty soon, a number of rumors about Gould sprang up in the Village. The most persistent rumor was that he had inherited a little money and had gone back to Massachusetts to live, and this gradually became the accepted explanation for his absence. A good many people did not believe this, I feel sure, or did not quite believe it, but they chose to appear to believe it, thereby washing their hands of Gould.

By and by, I told several people that Gould was in Pilgrim State. I told them in confidence. The first person I told was an old, old friend of Gould's named Edward Gottlieb, who was managing editor of the *Long Island Press*, a daily newspaper published out in Queens, at Jamaica. In his youth, Gottlieb had lived in the Village and had written poetry for little magazines and had hung out in bohemian joints, in one of which he had got acquainted with

Gould. After deciding that he wasn't a poet and never would be, he had become a newspaperman. He had worked for the *Press* for twenty-five years, progressing from reporter to city editor to managing editor, and at least once a month, and sometimes several times a month, during all those years, Gould had taken the subway out to Jamaica and had gone to his office and had got a contribution from him. I told Gottlieb for two reasons. He had called me a couple of times about Gould and sounded worried about him, and I felt guilty about not telling him. The principal reason I told him, however, was that I happened to know he knew a great deal about state mental hospitals. In 1943, he and his newspaper had done an investigation of Creedmoor State Hospital, in Queens Village, that had led to an improvement of conditions not only in Creedmoor but also in other state hospitals, including Pilgrim State, and Governor Dewey had appointed him to the Board of Visitors at Creedmoor. I had once had a talk with him about this investigation, and I knew that he had a number of friends in medical and administrative capacities at Pilgrim State, and it seemed to me that he was in a position to be very helpful to Gould.

Gottlieb said he would talk with his friends at Pilgrim State and do everything for Gould that he possibly could do. "The way it sounds," he said, "I'm afraid there isn't a hell of a lot that can be done. I'm afraid poor Joe is getting on down toward the end of the line."

From time to time thereafter, Gottlieb telephoned me and gave me news about Gould. "Joe's worst symptom is apathy," he said during one of these calls. "He mostly just sits and stares into the distance. However, every once in a while, the doctors say, something seem to stir in his mind and a smile comes on his face and he rouses himself and gets up and scampers around the ward and waves his arms up and down and makes strange, unearthly screeches until he wears himself out. He seems to be trying to communicate something with these screeches. The doctors and the nurses and the other patients don't know what he's doing, of course—they're completely mystified—but I know what he's doing, and I'm sure you do."

On Sunday, August 18, 1957, around eleven o'clock at night, Gottlieb telephoned me and said he had just been notified that Gould had died. We spoke for a few minutes about how sad it was, and then I asked him if Gould had left any papers.

"No," he said. "None at all. As the man at the hospital said, 'Not a scratch.' I was hoping that he had. I was particularly hoping that he had left some instructions about what he wanted done with the Oral History. He used to say that he wanted two-thirds of it to go to the Harvard Library and the other third to the Smithsonian Institution, but it doesn't seem right to split it up that way. When scholars start using it as source material, it will be a nuisance if they have to go up to Cambridge to see one part of it and then down to Washington to see some other part. Maybe one institution could be prevailed upon to relinquish its share to the other, and then it could be kept intact. By the way, where is the Oral History?"

I said that I didn't know.

Gottlieb's voice instantly became concerned. "I took it for granted that you knew," he said. "I took it for granted that Joe had told you."

I said that I didn't know where the Oral History was, and that I didn't know anybody who did know where it was.

"*Well,*" said Gottlieb, "we'll just have to start hunting for it. We'll just have to start telephoning and get in touch with all the people who knew him best and call a meeting and form a committee and get busy and start hunting for it. It's probably scattered all over. Some of it may still be stored in the cellar of that farmhouse near Huntington where he put it during the war—that stone cellar he was always talking about, the cellar on the duck farm—and some of it may be stored in the studios of friends of his in the Village, and some of it may be stored in storerooms in

some of those hotels and flophouses he lived in. Do flophouses have storerooms? They must. People must leave
things with the clerks in them for safe-keeping during the
night the same as they do in other hotels, and then go off
and forget all about them the same as they do in other hotels, and the flophouses must have to make some kind of
provision for this. I confess I have no idea where to start.
The first thing we'll need is a list of addresses of places he
lived in. Maybe you could start right now making such a
list. You will help with this, won't you? You will be on the
committee?"

I didn't know what to say. Gottlieb was an energetic
man, the kind of man who gets things done, and I could
tell by the way he talked that he was going to get to work
the first thing in the morning and start forming a committee, and that very soon the members of the committee
would be rummaging around in farmhouses all over Long
Island and in studios all over the Village and in flophouses
all over the Bowery. I could save him a lot of trouble if I
spoke up right then and told him what I knew about the
Oral History—I could save him and his committee quite
a wild-goose chase—but one of the few things I have
learned going through life is that there is a time and a
place for everything, and I didn't think that this was the
time or the place to be telling one of Joe Gould's oldest
friends that I didn't believe the Oral History existed. Joe

Gould wasn't even in his grave yet, he wasn't even cold yet, and this was no time to be telling his secret. It could keep. Let them go ahead and look for the Oral History, I thought. After all, I thought, I could be wrong. Hell, I thought—and the thought made me smile—maybe they'll find it.

Gottlieb repeated his question, this time a little impatiently. "You will be on the committee, won't you?" he asked.

"Yes," I said, continuing to play the role I had stepped into the afternoon I discovered that the Oral History did not exist—a role that I am only now stepping out of. "Of course I will."

(1964)

.